CLEAN IT!

Your All-Purpose Household Cleaning Guide

CLEAN IT!

Your All-Purpose Household Cleaning Guide

Edited by Jaala Weingarten

Original Research by Mary Jo Appel

Nelson Doubleday, Inc. • Garden City, New York

Copyright © 1983 by Nelson Doubleday, Inc.

No copyright is claimed on the U.S. Government
material that appears in this book.

All Rights Reserved
Printed in the United States of America
Design by Jeanette Portelli

The editors wish to express their thanks
to Kim Kingon for reviewing the manuscript.

Preface

This book is designed to serve as a handy reference for simple, effective methods to help solve most common household cleaning problems. Our advice and suggestions are aimed at busy people—many of whom are not full-time homemakers—who have neither the time nor the inclination to pore over cleaning encyclopedias and to stock up on elaborate, expensive equipment and supplies.

We have made a special effort to keep the cleaning instructions and recommendations concise and easy-to-follow, and to concentrate on the ones that have consistently proven their worth over the years. Some of the cleaning solution "recipes" are homemade. Neither today's technology nor the chemical industry that has endeavored to make cleaning chores less backbreaking has made these solutions obsolete. Most of our advice and suggestions are based on average housekeeping conditions, although we offer the answers to many special cleaning problems, too.

This practical guide provides, we believe, all the household cleaning solutions anyone—beginner or expert—needs to keep a home clean and easy to care for.

Contents

1. **Cleaning Products and Aids** 1

   Common Household Cleaners •
   Commercial Cleaners • Cleaning Tools •
   Safety Suggestions

2. **Home Appliances, Equipment, and Fixtures** 18

   Major Kitchen Appliances •
   Small Electric Kitchen Appliances •
   Cooling/Heating/Humidifying Equipment •
   Home Safety Equipment •
   Bathroom Fixtures and Furnishings •
   Lighting Fixtures

3. **Cookware and Tableware** 45

   Types of Cookware • Cutlery • Tableware

4. **Furniture** 61

   Types of Furniture •
   Special Finishes, Surfaces

5. **Decorative Objects and Collectibles** 70

   Accessories • Artwork •
   Fabric and Fiber Crafts •
   Books

6. **Floors and Floor Coverings** — 83

   Types of Floors • Carpets and Rugs •
   Home Carpet Cleaning

7. **Walls and Ceilings** — 98

   Painted Walls and Ceilings • Paneling •
   Papered Walls • Stain Removal

8. **Windows and Window Coverings** — 103

   Window Washing • Blinds • Curtains •
   Draperies • Screens • Shades

9. **Stain Removal** — 112

   General Procedures • Cleaning Solutions •
   Types of Stains

10. **Pest Control** — 119

    Preventive Measures • Pesticides •
    Types of Household Pests

    Index — 143

CLEAN IT!

Your All-Purpose Household Cleaning Guide

1. CLEANING PRODUCTS AND AIDS

To walk into an immaculate, clean-smelling house or apartment is always a pleasure; it makes you feel comfortable, relaxed. To keep a home that way, however, is hardly relaxing, most people will agree.

There is comfort in knowing that you are not alone in feeling that way. Help comes from a large home-care industry dedicated to keeping every room and corner of your home and its furnishings clean.

Even a cursory look through any supermarket reveals a variety of products for what seems to be every possible cleaning need. When shopping, take the time to carefully read the labels of different products to determine which best suits your cleaning purpose.

On the following pages, some of the most basic cleaning supplies are described, along with suggestions for making your own cleaning solutions. The second part of this chapter contains a convenient list of the basic cleaning tools needed to keep your household the way you want it to be—clean smelling, fresh, and comfortable to live in.

Cleaning Products

COMMON HOUSEHOLD CLEANERS

Household cleaners come in two basic forms: liquid and powder. Some are mild, for light duties; others are heavy duty, for tough cleaning jobs.

Baking Soda

This multipurpose product is gentle and will not scratch appliance and counter surfaces.

- Use baking soda to ease off burned food spots on porcelain enamel cookware, range and refrigerator surfaces, chrome trim, and appliance housings. Don't use baking soda on aluminum; it darkens the finish.
- To remove odors from carpets and rugs, sprinkle on some baking soda; then vacuum it up after waiting about 15 minutes. For persistent odors, wait overnight before vacuuming the baking soda from the rug.
- Clean and deodorize a food-chopping board by rubbing it with baking soda; then use a dampened cloth to clean the area.
- Put baking soda on stained coffee or tea cups, and use a dampened cloth to remove the stain.
- Take off the top of a box of baking soda; put the box in the refrigerator to absorb odors. Its drawing powers should be good for a month or two. Then empty the box of soda down the kitchen sink to freshen and clean the drain.
- Keep a large box of baking soda handy. In case of an accidental kitchen fire, you'll be prepared to douse the flames with it if a fire extinguisher is not within reach.

White Vinegar

This mild cleaner is also a good grease cutter. Use it for sparkling windows, chandeliers, etc., and for cleaning and brightening chrome and other metals.

- To make a window-cleaning solution, use 2 to 4 tablespoons of vinegar to 2 quarts of warm water. Use the same type of solution for cleaning glass shelves, glass tabletops, and mirrors.
- Use vinegar to remove light rust stains around the drains in the kitchen sink and in the bathtub. Saturate a cloth with vinegar and place it over the stain until you notice the rust lightening. Repeat if necessary.
- To periodically clean and clear a drain, heat a cup of vinegar, pour it into the drain and flush it down with hot water.
- To remove soap film and other grime on chrome faucets, dip a cloth in vinegar, then wipe the metal. Rinse in clear water and polish with a dry cloth.
- To remove tarnish from unlacquered brass or copper pieces, use a few tablespoons of salt with enough vinegar to dissolve it. Rub the mixture briskly over the tarnished items, then rinse in clear water. Polish dry.
- *Don't use vinegar on a marble surface.* Even though vinegar is a weak acid, any type of acid may etch marble.

Ammonia

This all-around, all-purpose, tough-job cleaner cuts through grease, grime, and heavy soil with quickness and ease. Always read the container label carefully before you buy household ammonia. There are different kinds: sudsy, clear, colored, and with fragrance added. When you decide to use ammonia, reread the label as a safety measure, to be certain it is exactly what you need for a specific purpose. Follow the recommendations on the container label for the advisable strength of ammonia to use.

- NOTE: When you uncap a bottle of ammonia, hold it away from your face so you will not inhale the fumes. Keep the room well ventilated when using ammonia, as the vapor can cause irritation to the eyes and nose, or even dizziness.
- Wear rubber gloves if you use a hot water and ammonia solution.
- Don't mix ammonia with chlorine bleach, or any other household chemical product. Don't combine it with a toilet bowl cleaner, a commercial oven cleaner, or a drain-cleaner product.
- Keep ammonia in its original container, clearly marked. Store it away from heat and in a well-ventilated place that children and pets cannot reach.
- To wash pots and pans that are unusually sticky with baked-on foods and grease, let them soak for 5 to 10 minutes in an ammonia solution before washing them. (Do not use ammonia when cleaning an aluminum surface.)
- To clean the glass window in an oven door, let it cool first; then wring a cloth out of a weak solution of ammonia and warm water, wipe the glass, rinse it in clear water, and use a fresh cloth to dry it thoroughly.
- When an oven is unusually soiled with baked-on grease and food spots, first let it cool completely before you clean it. One suggestion is to combine a cup of ammonia with a quart of warm water in a non-aluminum dish, and let the solution remain in the oven for at least eight hours, or overnight, to loosen

the soil. Another way is to put ammonia full-strength in a saucer in the oven for the same length of time before cleaning the baked-on grease away.

Washing (Sal) Soda

This heavy-duty all-purpose cleaner is a grease and stain remover, an effective water softener, and a practical laundry aid. Use it in the amounts recommended by the manufacturer on the container label. It can do many jobs. Among them, it will:
- Remove caked-on food from a greasy broiler pan, plus burned crusty stains on pots and pans (but do not use washing soda on aluminum);
- Clean garbage pails;
- Help to keep drains open.
- NOTE: For drains that are somewhat clogged, but not completely stopped up, here is a suggestion from a member of the Extension Service, U. S. Department of Agriculture: "If flushing with boiling water doesn't help your clogged drain, dissolve one pound of washing soda in three gallons of boiling water and pour this solution down the drain."

Bleach

Among household bleaches, two of the better-known types are chlorine and oxygen (a dry powder made with sodium perborate). Chlorine is more multipurpose and the stronger of the two. In the laundry it is a fabric whitener, a stain remover, and a disinfectant. It cannot be used on every kind of fabric, so be sure to check the container label. The oxygen type, a milder bleach, is not a whitener, and may be used on colored washables. Follow the manufacturer's directions on the container label.

In addition to the job it does in the laundry, chlorine bleach is also an all-purpose household cleaner, disinfectant, and deodorizer. It can help prevent mildew, as well as remove it. Some of its other uses are:
- To clean, disinfect and deodorize food-chopping boards;
- To clean and freshen garbage pails;
- To remove many stains from sinks and bathtubs (it will not remove rust from these areas);
- To use as a toilet bowl cleaner, alone, *not* with any chemical.
- NOTE: Don't use bleach on metals, especially aluminum; it can pit or discolor them. If it accidentally splashes on silver, wash it off immediately.

COMMERCIAL CLEANERS

These versatile cleaners do a lot to take some of the drudgery out of housecleaning. They range from mild to heavy duty, from fine powders to the gritty, coarse kind. Therefore, it is essential for you to read the label on any product container so you know where, how, and in what amount to use the proper cleaner.

Detergents
Three different types of detergents are described below.
- *Light Duty:* These mild detergents are designed to do light-cleaning tasks. They are used for washing dishes and delicate fabrics by hand, and for removing spots and stains.
- *Heavy Duty:* The products in this category are designed for doing the family laundry, including heavily

soiled items. They may also be used for general household-cleaning tasks.
• *Dishwasher:* These detergents are for use only in automatic dishwashers; they are too strong for hand dishwashing.

All-purpose Cleaners

These tough-duty products come in powders, liquids, sprays, and aerosols. They are used for many household chores, including cleaning painted walls and woodwork, plastics, metals, porcelain, and washable flooring.

Among the extra-strong chemical products are those that clean drains, ovens, and toilet bowls. Because these products contain poisonous and corrosive chemicals, they must be handled with care. Read the label on the container and take heed of its precautions. Many people prefer to try a milder cleaner first before using a stronger product.

• NOTE: These strong commercial preparations should not be mixed with each other or with other household cleaners (especially chlorine bleach or ammonia) except in cases where you are specifically instructed otherwise.
• Try not to spill the product onto another surface.
• Keep out of the reach of children and pets.
• To store, place in a well-ventilated area in the original container.
• When working with extra-strong cleaners, wear waterproof household gloves, either plastic or rubber. Buy them long enough to protect your wrists; you may wish to turn the gloves up, forming a cuff to catch any drips. Usually, the gloves will be easier to

put on and remove if they are lined. Sprinkling talcum on your hands also helps.

Cleansers

Powdered cleaners usually contain an abrasive and a bleach. In type, they range from very gentle to coarse. Cleansers supply scouring and polishing action; deodorize and disinfect; and aid in soil and stain removal.

Waxes and Polishes

These products come in solids, creams, aerosols, and sprays. They are either solvent-based (containing wax or oil) or water-based. They are designed to protect and shine wood, metals, leather, vinyl, marble, and other types of surfaces. Some have anti-tarnish ingredients; some are self-polishing and never require buffing.

Read the manufacturer's label carefully. Assure yourself that you have the right product for the finish you want to protect.

Cleaning Tools

The equipment you use to do basic cleaning tasks is listed on the following pages, along with suggestions for cleaning these household helpers.

Brooms

- Give any type of broom a good dipping in a pail of warm, sudsy water to clean it. Rinse in a pail of clear water, and repeat the rinsing until you get out all the suds. (It's easier to rinse a broom under running water, but it uses up more water.)

- Hang up the broom to let it dry, with the bristles pointing downward. To protect the bristles, never let a broom stand on them, whether it is wet or dry.
- If a broom does not have a hanging ring on its handle, you can find a screw-and-circle-type ring at hardware stores. Add it to the top of the broom's handle.

Dustpans

If you select an upright dustpan, make sure the handle is the right length to suit your height and comfort.
- To clean, wipe the dustpan and handle with a sudsy cloth, rinse, and dry. Hang it in your utility closet where it will be easy to find and where no one will trip over it.

Mops

Use a mop with a removable mophead, a mechanical squeezing device (that saves your hands and strength), and a handle that is convenient for you to manage.
- To get rid of a lot of dust and dirt on a *string mop*, shake it into a paper bag. Remove the mophead and wash it. To wash by hand, douse it up and down in warm sudsy water. Repeat in fresh suds, if necessary. Rinse thoroughly. Squeeze out as much water as possible; then fluff up the mop strands and let the mop air dry, outdoors if possible.
- For machine-washing a string mop, you may wish to put the mophead in a washable mesh bag to protect the strands, then wash it along with other dirty items such as cleaning cloths (that have not been used with solvents), and small scatter rugs. Use the dryer to dry the mophead. Wipe the mop handle and frame with a

sudsy cloth, then rinse and dry it. Replace the mophead and hang up the mop by its handle.
- To clean a *sponge mop,* remove the mophead and squeeze warm suds through it. If the mop is very dirty, repeat the procedure using fresh suds. Rinse well. Wipe the mop handle and frame with a sudsy cloth, rinse, and wipe dry. Replace the cleaned mophead in its frame. Hang the mop up by its handle when it is stored away.

Sponges
- To keep any sponge fresh and sweet-smelling, wash it right after each use (or at least, give it a good rinse).
- Wash a natural sponge in warm suds, squeezing it gently to get out all the dirt, then rinse thoroughly and air dry.
- You can put a number of cellulose sponges in a mesh bag and place it in the washing machine. Because the sponges should be kept away from heat, don't use the dryer for them; let them air dry.

Pails
To facilitate your cleaning, a pail should have enough width at the top so that a sponge mop will sink in easily, and it should not be too heavy to carry around. If there is a lot of cleaning to do, two pails are better than one: one for washing; the other for rinsing.
- Whether the pail is made of metal or plastic, it should be cleaned and wiped dry completely before it is stored, in order to prevent rust and mildew.

Brushes
- If the sturdy-bristled brushes you use in the kitchen and bathroom are filled with lint and string, use a

wide-toothed comb to run through the bristles and lift out the tangled mess.
- Another cleaning suggestion is to put two brushes in a container of suds at the same time. Rub them together, with lots of suds to brush out the dirt and debris. Rinse several times in clear warm water to be certain the brushes are free from any trace of suds. Usually these brushes can be hung up, and this is a good way to air dry them.
- For soft-bristled brushes used for gentler dusting jobs, dip them in warm suds, then rinse thoroughly. Many of these brushes do not have handles, so place them on a thick padding of toweling, bristles downward, to dry. The soft padding should prevent the bristles from getting out of shape.

Dusting and Cleaning Cloths

For household chores you'll need a variety of cloths. When you want to dust your furnishings, use a soft absorbent cloth that will hold onto the dust and not scatter it (such as old knitwear with all metal hooks removed). For heavy-duty jobs, a cloth (such as terry toweling) should hold moisture.
- To clean these cloths, put them in the washing machine and then into the dryer.
- NOTE: Whenever you use any product that contains a solvent, such as furniture wax or a dry-cleaning fluid, the cloths you use are soaked with the solvent and should be given special care. It is especially important that they be kept away from heat, and *not* stored in their solvent-soaked state.
- Either discard solvent-soaked cloths or, with plenty of ventilation, wash them by hand in good, rich, hot

suds. Dry out-of-doors. *Never* put them into the washer or dryer, as they could be a fire hazard.
- If you discard solvent-soaked cloths, don't put them in the incinerator. If you leave them for the handyman or the garbage collector, wrap the material in a newspaper with a note attached explaining what is inside the package.

Wax-applicator Pads

Made of various materials, these pads are removable and replaceable.
- You may wish to discard these pads after use. If not, wash them right away, before the wax hardens.
- Treat these wax-soaked pads as you would a solvent-soaked cleaning cloth: keep them away from a heat source; never store when dirty; and if you're going to wash them, do it in a well-ventilated room by hand (never in the washing machine) in plenty of hot suds. If possible, dry outdoors.

Chamois Cloths
- Gently hand wash a chamois in tepid water and light-duty soap. Suds it carefully; don't wring or pull it out of shape. Rinse in clear lukewarm water. Place on an absorbent towel and use the towel to gently squeeze out moisture. Place it flat on a fresh dry towel to dry. As the chamois begins to dry, use your fingers to manipulate it gently to soften it.
- Let a chamois air dry. Before storing a chamois, be sure that it is completely dry.

Carpet Sweepers
- Unless its brush is kept clean, the sweeper will not do an effective job and may not be able to move back

and forth easily. If a carpet sweeper's brush is removable, flip it out to clean it. Use strong shears to cut through any lint or other ravelings; remove them. Wash the brush in warm suds. Rinse in clear warm water, and let the brush air dry. Be sure that the brush is dry before you replace it.
* Empty the dustpans onto a newspaper. Wring a hand sponge out of sudsy water and wipe inside the dustpans, and the interior of the sweeper box. Use a fresh, dampened sponge to rinse, then wipe with a dry cloth.
* To clean the exterior of the sweeper, wring a sponge out of warm suds to wipe it clean, then rinse with another sponge, dampened in warm water. Wipe dry.
* Oil as directed in your owner's manual. Some carpet sweepers are permanently oiled at the factory; others need oiling about 4 or 5 times a year, depending upon the type of sweeper you have.

Vacuum Cleaners
* Never let the dust bag become overfull, whether it is a cloth bag or a disposable one. Follow the manufacturer's instructions, when available, for removing and replacing the dust bag.
* Don't turn on the vacuum cleaner unless the dust bag is in place.
* Inspect the hoses to see that nothing is clogging up the passageways. Here is one way to clear a hose: attach it to the exhaust end of the vacuum; hold the bag over the hose, then turn on the vacuum cleaner, and whatever is cluttering up the hose will be swept into the bag. (Never vacuum up live ashes or cigarette butts.)
* At regular intervals, check the revolving brush for any buildup of lint or other materials that might im-

pede a smooth performance, and remove it. Replace cleaning brushes when worn.
- If your cleaner has a filter, check its condition occasionally to see if it needs cleaning or replacing.
- Check the condition of the belt. Replace if necessary.
- Take the model number of your machine along with you when you want to replace any parts.
- Don't use a defective power cord. If you notice it is frayed or worn, replace it right away. To protect the power cord, and yourself, don't run the machine over it while it is plugged in. Before attaching the cleaner's accessories, unplug the power cord from the wall outlet. To unplug, always take hold of the plug; *never* pull on the cord.
- To protect the mechanical parts inside the machine, don't begin to vacuum until you have picked up any hazardous-looking objects, such as a nail, an open safety pin, or any metallic object that could cause serious damage.
- To clean the vacuum's exterior, wipe it with warm water and mild detergent suds. Rinse and wipe dry.

ATTACHMENTS: Here are some specific vacuum cleaner attachments and their functions. A *general dusting brush* can clean upholstered draperies. A *furniture nozzle* will get into the seams of furniture cushions and mattresses. A *floor brush* cleans hard-surface flooring as well as walls. A soft *dusting brush* can clean hard-surface furniture, books, lamp bases and other lighting fixtures, plus display pieces used as room accessories. The *crevice tool* draws dust out of dresser drawers, cleans the spaces between large kitchen appliances, and gets into difficult-to-reach areas on a radiator.
- Keep all brushes and other attachments clean by

washing them in warm suds, then rinsing. Metal parts should not be submerged in water. Wipe them clean with a sudsy cloth or sponge.
• Be sure to let all attachments dry completely. Store them along with your vacuum cleaner in a dry place.

Safety Suggestions

In addition to the specific advice given on the previous pages for each cleaning product and cleaning tool, here are additional safety measures for you and your family to observe.

Emergency Telephone Numbers
• Keep the numbers of your doctor, fire and police departments, local ambulance service, and poison-control center near your telephone.

Fire Extinguisher
• Reserve a special place for a compact fire extinguisher in your home, not too close to your kitchen area, but handy enough so you can reach it quickly and easily if an emergency arises.
• Occasionally reread the directions on how to use the fire extinguisher so you'll never be caught unprepared.

Labeling Cleaning Products
• Always read the label on any cleaning product before you use it. Especially be aware of those labels that read "Poison," "Danger," "Warning," or "Caution." Do not store any of these under the kitchen sink or in

the bathroom where they are readily accessible to children.
- Never store a cleaning product on a shelf with your food supplies.
- Rearrange your storage space so you'll be able to keep the above labeled products in a locked, ventilated cabinet, or on shelves high enough to be beyond a child's reach.

Flammable Liquids

The flammable liquids to keep away from heated areas, or a heat source, include gasoline, kerosene, naphtha, dry-cleaning fluid, paint thinner, turpentine, linseed oil, hair spray in an aerosol can, and any chemical product that contains a flammable solvent. (Always check the label to be informed about the container's contents.)
- Keep all the above products in their original containers with the labels clearly showing. This is most important in the case of gasoline, which should never be stored in the house.
- Avoid using any flammable liquid near a pilot light or an open flame. Don't store it in an overheated area, or near a gas water heater or an oil burner.

Cord Care

For safety's sake, keep electrical cords in good condition. The letters UL (Underwriters Laboratories) should appear on the cord (as well as on the appliance). This indicates that the product meets the electrical safety standards. Underwriters Laboratories is a non-profit organization doing public safety laboratory testing on behalf of consumer and business groups.

(It sets safety standards, sometimes with government participation.)
- Don't let the electrical cord of any appliance dangle off a kitchen counter or run across the surface of a range.
- Keep oil and grease away from cords.
- To disconnect a cord, grasp the plug to pull it out. Do not pull on the cord line.
- Don't place a cord under a rug where it can be stepped on, or across a threshold.
- Don't bend a cord at a sharp angle. To store it, roll it up loosely, or hang it on a storage rack away from excessive heat. A cord should be kept in a relatively cool place.
- Never plan to have an electrical outlet in the kitchen too close to the sink or the top of the range. A portion of the cord length could fall into a water-filled sink or onto a hot range surface.
- Don't use a multi-outlet plug or overload a circuit by having too many appliances plugged into one outlet.
- Pay careful attention to the safety instructions in your owner's manual when a major appliance is equipped with a three-prong grounding plug that connects with a standard three-prong (grounding) electrical outlet. If in doubt, ask a qualified electrician.

2. HOME APPLIANCES, EQUIPMENT, AND FIXTURES

Major Kitchen Appliances

To obtain maximum performance and enjoyment from your household appliances, you should learn the correct way to care for and clean them. Whether you're buying a costly item such as a dishwasher or a less expensive appliance such as a toaster, always read and file the instruction booklet that comes with it. You'll be able to refer to it later for specific manufacturer's suggestions regarding its operation and care.

Dishwashers
In general, every time you use the dishwasher it leaves its interior clean. However, here are some general cleaning suggestions:
- To remove hard-water film, use vinegar during the wash action, or a rinse additive.

- While it isn't necessary to rinse dishes before placing them in the dishwasher, to prevent drain clogging, scrape the dishes well to remove any hard objects such as bones, fruit pits, nuts, and cocktail picks.
- Before washing tableware, remove any large lumps of starchy foods or any substance that will not dissolve easily in water. Unless your dishwasher has a special cycle to remove scorched or crusty baked-on foods from cooking utensils, soak each utensil in hot water, then get rid of the excess with a plastic scrubber.
- To keep the seal around the door or lid of the dishwasher clean, mix 3 tablespoons of baking soda with 1 quart of warm water, dip a cloth in this solution, and wipe the area thoroughly.
- Periodically, apply a creamy polish (such as Jubilee) to the dishwasher's exterior. It will protect it, as well as keep it clean and shined.

Refrigerators, Freezers

Specific instructions are needed to help you clean and care for a refrigerator or a freezer that uses any of the three basic defrosting systems:

Manual-defrost refrigerators with a single door and a small frozen-food storage compartment at the top (inside the refrigerator unit).

Cycle-defrost refrigerators with a separate compartment for the freezer, generally located above the refrigerator. Manual defrosting is required in the freezer but not in the refrigerator which defrosts automatically.

No-frost refrigerators that eliminate visible frost accumulation; manual defrosting is not necessary.

To keep your refrigerator free from odors, defrost it whenever the ice has built up to ¼ inch in thickness.

REFRIGERATOR INTERIOR:
- To defrost, turn the control to "off" and unplug the electric cord of the refrigerator (if possible) before cleaning. You must not unplug the electric cord while the appliance is running.
- Take out of the refrigerator cabinet all removable parts such as the shelves, food containers, and accessories. Wash them in mild suds; then rinse and dry.
- Don't try to speed up the defrosting process by chipping at the frost with a sharp tool or utensil. Instead, place a container of very hot water in the freezer compartment, and several others in the refrigerator cabinet. Close the refrigerator door at once. Replace with new containers of hot water as the first ones cool.
- Clean the interior of the refrigerator after it is defrosted. Use a solution of 2 tablespoons of baking soda to 1 quart of water. Never use harsh cleansers of any kind as they could scratch the interior's finish. Use a small stiff brush to get into the cabinet's corners. Dip the brush into the washing solution and ease off any dried-on food spills. Rinse and dry.
- Wash the door seal or gasket (the rubber edge that goes around the door inside the refrigerator) to keep it free of grease and dirt. If this accumulates, the door will not close tightly and the cool air will escape. With a sponge, wash the gasket and door liner with a soda-water solution (see above) to get rid of any grease buildup. Rinse well in clear, warm water; then dry thoroughly. Never use any harsh cleansers; they could harm the rubber seal.
- Replace the cleaner shelves and accessories.

REFRIGERATOR EXTERIOR:
- Wash the outside cabinet with warm water and a light-duty detergent. Check your owner's manual for recommendations on what to use for your refrigerator's exterior finish. Harsh scouring powders should not be used.
- Keep the condenser coils clean. Refrigerators with condenser coils at the rear of the cabinet only need a casual dusting whenever you clean behind them. However, to maintain peak performance of the appliance, clean the condenser thoroughly at least twice a year—in the spring and in the fall.
- Bottom-mounted condenser coils get dusty faster and need cleaning more often. (Check your owner's manual for the best way to reach these coils for cleaning.) The dusting-tool attachment of your vacuum cleaner or a long-handled brush may be used to remove dirt from the condenser.
- NOTE: Never use one electric appliance to clean another when *both* are drawing power.

After the interior and exterior of the refrigerator have been cleaned, rinsed, and dried, plug the cord back into the wall outlet and return the temperature control to its original setting. Let the refrigerator chill before replacing all frozen and refrigerated foods.

Ranges

Your range won't work at its best if you don't keep it clean. It will also use up more energy if its working parts are clogged with dirt. Ranges vary in design. Since special features for easier cleaning have been added to both electric and gas ranges, you should consult the specific cleaning instructions in the owner's manual for your particular model.

ELECTRIC RANGES: Turn off the heating units and let the range get comfortably cool before doing any cleaning. To avoid a buildup of spills and spots, clean your range after every use. This could mean no more than a sudsy wipe with a cloth or sponge over the surface and around the heating elements (without getting them wet), then a quick rinse with clean water and thorough drying.

- Blot up spillovers as soon as possible. For stubborn spots caused by food spills, soak a cloth with household ammonia, place it over the spot, and close the oven door for about 30 minutes. Remove the cloth, dip it in warm suds, and wipe off the spot. Baking soda sprinkled on for five minutes is fine to remove less stubborn spots.
- Scorched, dried-on food spots should come off by nudging them with a nylon pad, such as Dobie (it's less harsh on the range surface), sudsed in warm water, plus a light-duty detergent. Or use a fine grade of a nonabrasive cleaner, such as powdered whiting, and rub it on the burned-on spill with a dampened cloth. (Large all-purpose paint and housewares stores should have various grades of powdered whiting. Get the *fine* grade.) Never use anything abrasive, such as harsh scouring pads and powders.
- To burn off food spills on the heating element, turn it to high. Use a soft brush to get rid of tiny burned fragments after the element has cooled. On some ranges you can unplug the unit for easy cleaning, but never put the surface heating element in water. Keep the pans under the heating element clean; most are removable.
- When the whole oven needs a thorough cleaning, pour about ½ cup of household ammonia into a

small bowl and place it in a *cold* oven. Keep the oven door closed for about 4 hours, or overnight, to soften any stubborn food spills and baked-on grime. Then remove the bowl (along with the oven racks for later cleaning) and add the ammonia to about a quart of warm water. Dip a cloth or sponge in this solution and clean the entire oven, including the interior side of the oven door. Next, wash the oven and door with a cloth or sponge dipped in warm detergent suds, then use clear warm water to rinse all areas. Wipe the oven dry. Before returning the racks to the oven, wash them in sudsy water, rinse, and dry completely.

- To prevent layers of cold grease from building up, clean the broiler pan and the insert grid after it is used. When it has had a chance to cool a bit, while wearing household gloves, you should remove the broiler assembly and pour the grease into a container. After the grease is removed and the broiler grid and pan are cool, it helps to let them soak in a solution of light-duty detergent and hot water. Then use a scouring pad to remove any burned-on foods that don't soak off.

GAS RANGES: Cleaning a gas range surface is quite similar to cleaning an electric range top surface. The heat must be turned off and the range surface should be cool. Spillovers should be wiped up at once. Harsh scouring powders should never be used.

- Begin with a cool oven. If the door lifts off for easier oven cleaning, place it flat, face down for safety, in an out-of-the-way area. Wash the door on both sides in warm suds, then rinse and dry. If the oven door has a glass window, wash it with a weak solution of household ammonia and water. Rinse and dry thoroughly.

- Wash the oven interior with a cloth or sponge wrung out of warm detergent solution. Rinse the cloth in warm water, and wipe the interior; then dry the inside of the oven.
- A nonabrasive way to clean burned-on oven spills is to cover the area with baking soda and let it remain there at least 5 minutes. Then rub the spot with a damp cloth to loosen up the spill. Rinse with clear warm water and dry.
- For a more complete cleaning, leave a bowl of ammonia overnight in a cold oven. When you finish your cleaning the next morning, follow the ammonia treatment suggestions for a thorough going over of electric ovens.

Control Knobs: If these are not removable, use a skinny percolator or bottle brush, well sudsed, to clean them.

Surface Burners: Remove the utensil supports or grates; lift out burner bowls and burner rims, if possible. Take out the drip pans. When dismantling burners, put in an orderly manner for reassembly. If you clean your range every day, you should only have to clean away food fragments on burners with a stiff brush, then wipe with a damp cloth and dry. Otherwise, mix ½ cup of detergent in 1 gallon of hot water and suds the grates, burners, and trays. Rinse and dry.

- Another suggestion for periodic cleanups is to remove the burner assembly and wash in a solution of 1 cup of ammonia to 1 gallon of hot water.
- Next, check the burner head (cap). If the holes are clogged, use a wire brush or fine wire to open them.
- Wash the area under the cleaned drip pans before replacing them. Some ranges have a lift-up top to

make it easy to reach this space. Otherwise, get underneath with a long-handled kitchen brush.

Gas Broiler: Clean the broiler pan right after you use it. Empty it of grease and let the broiler pan and grill cool a bit before immersing them in the sink to soak in warm water and a liquid detergent.

Microwave Ovens
- Before cleaning, turn off the power and give the oven a chance to cool. Clean the interior, door, and seals with a cloth or sponge wrung out of warm water and a light-duty detergent. Rinse and dry. Do the same for the exterior of the oven.
- Do not use scouring pads, steel wool, or other abrasives to clean a microwave oven.

GLASS-CERAMIC RANGES: A glass-ceramic smooth-top panel for a range (Pyroceram[R] by Corning Glass) with special heating circuits under it has been developed with especially strengthened glass to withstand high heat. Read and follow the precise usage instructions provided by the range manufacturer.
- A *cleaner-conditioner,* made especially for the glass-ceramic cooktop, is available from your range dealer. Follow the directions on the container's label.
- Wipe up any food spills or liquid splatters at once. When the cooktop is hot, use several clean dry paper towels to blot up the spills. Never use wet paper towels since their wetness could cause a steam burn.
- Clean your *cooled* cooktop daily. Avoid harsh cleansing powders, metal pot cleaners, or abrasive scouring pads. Use a fine, non-scratchy cleaning powder (such as Bon Ami Polishing Cleanser) and a

moistened nylon pad or a non-scratching scrubber sponge (such as Scrunge).
- Remove burned-on food from a cooled area with a single-edge razor blade, held so that the entire edge is away from your body, at about a 30° angle. It is easier if the blade is in a razor holder, the type used to scrape paint from glass.

OVEN-CLEANING SYSTEMS: If you have a self-cleaning or continuous-cleaning oven, be sure to follow the exact instructions of the manufacturer regarding its care.

Self-cleaning Oven: Wipe off the oven frame and the part of the door liner that is outside the oven seal before using the self-cleaning mechanism. These areas are not reached during cleaning, but they do get enough heat to bake on grease and make it harder to remove later.

Continuous-cleaning Oven: First, try to blot up and remove all the excess spills with a paper towel or sponge. If this isn't possible, allow the oven to completely cool, then spray the soiled area with an all-purpose spray-on/wipe-off cleaner, such as Fantastik. Rub the cleaner into the surface with a nylon net pad. Let the spray remain on for 15–30 minutes. Scrub the soiled area again with a nylon brush or pad. Rinse or sponge thoroughly with cold water. Then set the oven to 475° F., and leave for 2 hours during which the continuous-cleaning process should eliminate any residue.

RANGE HOODS: Check your owner's manual for special suggestions to clean your type of range hood ventilator. In general:
- Turn off the fan, then turn off the power. Let the fan

cool a bit. Clean the fan blades with a cloth dampened in warm suds. Use a small brush or cotton swab to dig into corners and hard-to-reach places. To rinse, dampen a clean cloth in clear warm water and use another clean cloth to dry thoroughly.
- Wash the filter in warm detergent suds. Rinse and wipe dry. Wash any type of filter according to your owner's manual.
- Wash the outside surface with detergent and warm water, rinse, and dry.
- NOTE: Before using a commercial oven cleaner, read the label carefully. Many types contain lye or caustic soda which are toxic ingredients. You should avoid breathing their fumes, and don't let any of the cleaner spill on your hands. Wear moisture-proof gloves when using it. Also, avoid spilling a lye or caustic soda product on chromium or aluminum.

Small Electric Kitchen Appliances

The function of the appliance, its physical composition, and its type of finish are factors that determine what cleaning method to use. Here are some general instructions:
- Turn an appliance with an electric motor assembly to the "off" position, then unplug it before cleaning.
- Keep the motor assembly out of water unless the manufacturer specifies that it is safe to do so.
- Keep the power off, and the element unplugged, before you remove or add any accessory.
- Always keep appliances covered when not in use.

Decorative covers, available in department stores and housewares stores, will keep out dust and grime.

The following pages include some of the many small electric appliances on the market. The owner's manual you'll receive when purchasing these items will give you additional information for cleaning your specific type of appliance.

Blenders
- Clean a blender as soon after each use as possible. The manufacturer's instructions will tell which of the blender's parts are dishwasher safe, and it will give exact directions on how to clean the appliance.
- To remove sticky or solid foods from the food container, turn the appliance "off" and unplug it. Take the container off its base and fill it half-full with hot water and a light-duty detergent. Replace the cover; place the container on its base. Plug in the blender, turn it to a low speed, and let it blend for about 30 seconds. Then turn the blender to "off," unplug it, and take the container from the motor base. Empty it out, rinse it thoroughly in hot water, and dry it.
- Wash the blender's sealing ring, cutting blades, and lid in hot suds. Rinse well in clear hot water and dry.
- Do not immerse the motor base in water. Do not use harsh scouring powders. Wiping the motor base with a damp cloth, then polishing it with a dry cloth should be sufficient.

Electric Can Openers
- Remove the can opener's plug from the wall outlet before cleaning. If the can opener has an "off" switch, turn it off before unplugging.
- Remove the cutting wheel and the magnetic lid

catcher, if possible. Wash both quickly in hot suds, rinse thoroughly, and dry.
- Don't place the motor casing in water.
- Wipe the can opener's exterior with a damp, well-sudsed cloth. Use a mild nonabrasive cleanser for removing any stubborn spots. Use clear hot water to rinse; then wipe dry.

Electric Coffee Pots
- Always remove used coffee grounds immediately after each use (after the pot has cooled). If there is no time to wash the pot thoroughly, at least rinse it well.
- Unplug any electric coffee pot before washing it. If it has an "on-off" switch, turn it to "off," then unplug the cord from the wall outlet. If your coffee pot doesn't have an "on-off" switch, but does have a detachable cord, unplug the cord from the wall *before* pulling the cord from the appliance.
- Don't put the heating base of an electric coffee pot in water unless the manufacturer specifically says it is safe to do so.
- Scrub the basket of the coffee-grounds holder with a brush. Use a narrow brush to clean the coffee spout and inside the center stem. Use a plastic scrubber to clean inside the pot. Rinse all items well and dry.
- Here's a successful homemade cleaning solution to remove rancid coffee-oil stains from the interior of an electric percolator: add ½ cup white vinegar to 1 quart water. Pour it in a cleaned percolator. Let the solution percolate for at least 2 minutes. Pour off the cleaning solution. Wash the interior of the percolator and its parts with hot suds. *Do not immerse the pot* in water unless your owner's manual states

that it is safe to do so. Rinse, then dry all parts completely before reassembling.
- Avoid using harsh cleansers to remove spots or splatters on the outside of a coffee pot.

Food Processors
- Before cleaning, turn the switch to "off," unplug the processor, and *don't remove the processor's lid* or reach into the bowl until the blades have come to a *full stop*. (This may take from 4–15 seconds, depending upon the appliance.)
- Remove the bowl from its base, empty it of food, and take the processor apart, following the manufacturer's instructions carefully. Check to see which parts are dishwasher safe. In general, the bowl (usually see-through plastic) and other removable parts may be washed in hot suds, rinsed, and dried.
- Do not immerse the section containing the motor in water. Wipe the outside of the processor with a damp cloth. Use a dry cloth to polish.

Electric Frypans
- To avoid a buildup of grease-type stains that may be impossible to remove, clean the inside and outside of your frypan after each use.
- For any type of electric frypan, first turn the switch to "off," unplug the cord from the outlet, and then remove the cord from the pan. Let the frypan cool.
- Don't place the frypan in water unless your owner's manual permits this. (*Never,* when the thermostat is attached.) Wash the pan's interior and exterior with hot suds; then rinse and dry. Wash its cover in the same way.

- Don't use scratchy scouring cleansers, abrasive metal pads, or steel wool on a non-stick interior.
- To eliminate hard-to-remove stains, use only a cleaning pad or cloth which states "safe for cleaning non-stick finishes." One type is a nylon mesh cleaning pad. To use, wet the pad in hot light-duty detergent suds and gently rub away stubborn stains. Rinse the frypan with clear warm water and dry.

Electric Mixers

Today's mixers and their attachments vary from one manufacturer to another. It is in your own best interest to read the manufacturer's instructions about cleaning and caring for your specific mixer.

STANDING MIXERS:
- Don't remove an attachment until you have turned it "off" and unplugged the motor base from the outlet. Then wash the attachment in hot suds, rinse in clean hot water, and dry thoroughly.
- Bowls made of heat-resistant glass or stainless steel, and the mixer's beaters, may be washed in an automatic dishwasher. However, when stainless-steel bowls are left to air dry, they may spot. It's best to hand dry them with a soft cloth as soon as possible.
- Some manufacturers of highly polished stainless bowls suggest that you hand wash them since some strong detergents in the automatic dishwasher, plus high heat and hard minerals in the water, can dull the finish. Use a light-duty detergent in warm water, rinse thoroughly, and dry immediately.
- Never immerse the motor base in water. Don't use harsh cleaning powders on the motor base. Wipe it

with a sudsy cloth or sponge. If necessary, use a slim brush for hard-to-reach areas.
- For stubborn spots, mix baking soda with just enough water to make a paste, then use a damp cloth to ease off the spots on the mixer's base. To rinse, wipe with a cloth wrung out of clear warm water, and polish it dry with a fresh clean cloth.

HAND MIXERS:
- To clean, turn the mixer "off," then unplug it from the wall outlet. The beaters are easy to remove and easy to clean. Some are chrome-plated; others are stainless steel. Wash the beaters by hand or in the dishwasher.
- Don't place the body of the mixer, which holds the motor, in water, and don't use abrasive cleansers to clean it. Wipe the body of the mixer with a sudsy cloth. Rinse by wiping it with a cloth wrung out of clear water, and dry.

Pressure Cookers
- Do not immerse the cooker's cover in water after you have removed it, as this could harm the sensitive items, such as the vent pipe and dial gauge, held within the cover. Use a cloth wrung out of sudsy water to wipe the cover. Rinse it with a cloth dampened in clear water; then dry it.
- The vent pipe in the cover, which allows excess pressure to be released, can be cleaned with a very narrow brush or a pipe cleaner. This will brush away food particles and clean the vent's narrow opening.
- Regularly clean the sealing ring, which fits into the cooker's cover and forms a pressure-tight seal between the cover and the body of the pressure cooker. Wash

the sealing ring in warm suds, rinse, and dry it. Use a small, stiff brush to clean out the groove in the cooker's lid before replacing the sealing ring.
- Check your owner's manual to learn which of the parts are removable and may be washed safely. If you have an electric heat-control cooker, keep it out of water.
- Never wash an empty, overheated cooker until it has cooled. Don't pour cold water into it to speed up cooling; this might damage the metal. Wash the cooker (body) in light-duty detergent suds and warm water. Rinse in clear warm water and dry well.

Electric Slicing Knives

Since models of electric knives differ in makeup (some are cordless), it's a good idea to refer to your owner's manual for special-care instructions. Here are some basic suggestions:
- To clean, unplug the knife cord from the outlet before you detach the cord from the knife handle.
- Don't immerse the knife handle in water or any other liquid, since the motor that powers the knife is housed in the handle.
- Remove the blades from the handle and wash them in hot suds. Rinse and dry thoroughly. To clean the knife handle, use a cloth dampened in clear water to wipe away any food soil, and then dry with a fresh cloth.

Electric Skillets and Woks

Since various metals are used to make electric skillets and woks, specific care directions may vary, so consult the manufacturer's booklet. Here are some general instructions:

- Let the appliance cool down normally. Don't rush this process by adding cold water; the appliance might warp. Turn the switch to "off," then unplug it from the wall outlet, and disconnect the heat-control cord from the cooled appliance.
- Wash with a sponge and hot suds, rinse well, and dry.
- For stubborn stains, use a gentle, nonabrasive nylon scrubber or plastic scouring pad to ease off the stain.

Toasters
- Unplug the toaster and let it cool before cleaning.
- Remove the crumb tray, if possible. If it isn't removable, use a long, slim brush to reach any crumbs. (You can turn some toaster models upside down to get the toast crumbs out.) Clean the tray with a cloth dampened in warm suds, rinse it, and dry well.
- Never put the toaster in water.
- Clean the chrome-plated exterior after each use by wiping it with a damp cloth. About once a week wipe with a sudsed cloth or sponge, rinse well, and dry. Any food spots can be eased off by putting some baking soda or fine-powdered whiting on a damp cloth.

Toaster-broilers
Many of these appliances are continuous-cleaning. Here are some general suggestions to keep them looking their best:
- Avoid using harsh cleansers, scratchy scouring pads, and spray-on cleaners.
- Wipe up excessive spills as soon as possible. A sponge dampened in warm suds, followed by a rinse and drying, is all that's usually needed to clean the interior if it's done after each use.
- For stubborn stains, use a cleaning pad that scours

without scratching to clean the oven tray, racks, and interior oven. (Be sure that the appliance is unplugged and cool before you begin to clean it.) Dampen the pad first, then generously sprinkle baking soda on it and rub off the baked-on stains. Rinse with a dampened cloth, then dry.
- Usually the broiler window may be cleaned with a liquid dishwashing detergent and warm water, then rinsed well to prevent streaking, and polished dry with a soft cloth. If the door's window glass has turned brownish in color from smoke, use *undiluted* dishwashing detergent and rub it gently with a non-scratching plastic cleaning pad. Rinse with a cloth dampened in clear water, and polish dry with a soft, clean cloth. (Some manufacturers recommend using a commercial window-glass cleaner for difficult stains on the oven window. Follow the directions on the container's label.)

Cooling/Heating/Humidifying Equipment

Air-conditioners
- Turn the unit off and disconnect the air-conditioner before you begin to clean it.
- Take off the front panel and place it on a newspaper on a flat surface. Manufacturers suggest using the dusting tool of your vacuum to clean the panel.
- Remove the air filter. Usually the filter is located behind a hinged or removable front panel on the indoor side of the unit. Different materials are used to

make filters: some are self-cleaning, some are disposable, others are reusable.
- In general, the filter should be cleaned or changed once a month, more often if you live in a high-pollution area. If your unit has a reusable filter, suds it gently, then rinse in clear warm water. Squeeze the filter to remove excess water; then replace it, while damp (unless otherwise directed by your owner's manual). If you change filters, make sure the replacement is the same material and thickness.
- Clean the condenser coils whenever they are dirty. While the air-conditioner is unplugged, use the dusting tool of your vacuum cleaner to remove dust and dirt from these cooling coils.
- Make sure that no liquid gets into the motor, electrical control box, or compressor electrical terminals.
- When you turn the unit off, wait at least 2–3 minutes before turning it back on or it may blow a fuse.

CENTRAL AIR-CONDITIONING SYSTEM: Keep careful watch over the condition of the air filter in a central air-conditioning system; it will lose efficiency if allowed to run while the filter is dirty. A dirty filter can also cause compressor failure. Most manufacturers recommend that you clean the filter when it gets dirty, which could be every other month in some homes.
- Some central systems have disposable filters, although washable permanent filters are also available. One permanent type of filter is made of aluminum which can be washed in detergent suds, rinsed, and dried. (When these need replacing, they are available in air-conditioning supply shops and in some hardware stores.)

- *Never* operate your air-conditioning system without a filter. (It traps soot, dirt, dust, and pollen.)

Electric Fans
- Unplug and let it cool before you start your cleaning.
- The fan should be dusted regularly. When not in use, keep a cover on it. When necessary, wipe the blades and the motor casing with a cloth wrung out of warm soapy water. Rinse in clean warm water and dry completely. Never operate a fan unless it is thoroughly dried.

Humidifiers
- How you clean your humidifier depends upon its particular type; how often you clean it depends upon the water hardness in your area and the speed at which slimy mineral deposits accumulate. You may need to clean your humidifier only once a year, or it may need attention every two weeks. Check the manufacturer's instruction booklet.

Dehumidifiers
- Whichever model you have, empty the pan as often as necessary; check daily. Wash the interior with warm light-duty detergent suds. This is to prevent mold, mildew, or bacteria growth.

Home Safety Equipment

Smoke Detectors
- Dirt, extreme changes in temperature, and cooking exhaust smoke can cause a false alarm or a malfunc-

tion of a smoke detector. Keep the front cover of the unit clean. Usually it is removable and can be washed with a sponge in hot suds. Rinse in clear water and dry thoroughly. (When the cover is off, be careful not to touch any portion of the unit's interior.) Replace the detector's cover immediately after cleaning.
- Try to keep dust from building up on the unit's interior mechanism. At regular intervals use the small brush attachment of your vacuum cleaner to dust the grillwork, slots, or open area (on the detector's cover above the alarm system).
- When you buy a smoke detector you should receive detailed instructions on how to care for it. If you do not have these directions and have any questions about your alarm system, call your local dealer, or the office of your city's fire commissioner.

Bathroom Fixtures and Furnishings

A sparkling-clean bathroom is the result of simple daily care plus a few periodic extra cleanups.

Bathtubs, Wash Basins, and Countertops
- Since most of these are made of porcelain or laminate, harsh abrasives or scouring powders, which could scratch the finish, should be avoided.
- To clean, wash with a sponge or a soft cloth dipped in detergent and warm water, or a chemical cleaner sold for this purpose. Rinse and dry. For stubborn stains, a mild cleansing powder can be used, and then rinse thoroughly.
- The scummy "bathtub ring" that results from soap

residue, most often in hard-water areas, can be removed with an all-purpose cleaner on a damp sponge. To prevent this buildup of soap scum, add a special water conditioner to the water when taking a bath.
- Rust spots, unless they have penetrated into the porcelain surface, can be removed by rubbing the spot with a cut lemon and rinsing thoroughly. Another rust-removal solution is a mixture of borax powder and lemon juice.
- A heavily stained bathtub or sink can be cleaned by rubbing in a paste made of a few drops of hydrogen peroxide and cream of tartar, or use a special rust remover made for porcelain.

Toilet Bowls
- For a routine cleaning inside the bowl, use an all-purpose detergent solution or a cleaner made especially for the purpose.
- Use a long-handled cleaning brush to scrub all interior surfaces, particularly under the rim and in the trap.

Faucets, Shower Heads, and Chromium-plated Fittings
- Wash these fittings with a sponge and sudsy warm water; dry immediately to restore their sheen. You can remove any hard-water or soap-scum spots by rubbing them with vinegar.
- All fittings, whether chromium or nickel-plated, can be washed with sudsy warm water, rinsed, and towel-dried.

Mirrors and Windows
- Use a mild cleanser to clean bathroom mirrors or windows. An effective solution is 2 tablespoons of

household ammonia to 2 quarts of warm water; or you can use 2–4 tablespoons of vinegar to 2 quarts of warm water.
- If you use a spray cleaner, spray it on a lint-free cloth first to avoid any dripping. Polish with a chamois to avoid streaks. (See also Chapter 8, "Windows and Window Coverings.")

Bathroom Walls

Most of the wall area will need only an occasional wiping with a damp or sudsy cloth.
- To remove the film caused by soap and hard-water elements that appear on glazed ceramic tile or other wall coverings, scrub the wall surface with a mild detergent solution or with a water-conditioner. A spray-on tile and bathroom cleaner can also be used. Many of these are also disinfectants.
- To remove a more stubborn film accumulation, use an all-purpose liquid or spray cleaner and scrub with a stiff-bristled brush. Rinse the surface, then rub it dry with a clean cloth or towel to make it sparkle. The tiles will also regain their gleam if you wipe them with a sponge dipped in ammonia and water.
- For quick touch-ups, wipe down bathroom walls with just a sponge mop and detergent, then rinse.

Bathroom Floors
- Ceramic tile should be damp-mopped as part of a regular routine. Wash the floor, when necessary, with an all-purpose cleaner, or washing soda and warm water. Use a nonabrasive cleanser on stubborn spots. Rinse carefully and wipe dry.
- Resilient flooring, such as vinyl, vinyl-asbestos, and

linoleum should be washed and waxed regularly. Mop with an all-purpose liquid detergent and warm water. Polish with a water-based self-polishing or buffing wax. (See also Chapter 6, "Floors and Floor Coverings.")

Shower Curtains
- These are usually plastic and wash easily in warm water suds (about 4 minutes in the washing machine). Remove before the spin cycle and hang them on their hooks to dry. Since shower curtains attract mildew, spray them with a disinfectant after they are dry.
- Shower curtains other than plastic can usually be washed safely in mild, lukewarm soapsuds. Look for their instruction label.

Bathmats
- Soak bathmats in a mild solution of bleach and water. If necessary, use a brush (but not a stiff one) to get rid of soil and grime.

Lighting Fixtures

Bulbs (incandescent)
- Turn off the light switch and unplug the cord. Let the bulb cool before wiping off the dust.
- Hold the bulb by the end made of metal so you won't get it wet when washing. Wring a clean cloth out of warm sudsy water to clean the bulb. To rinse, wring a fresh cloth out of clear warm water. Dry completely.

Fluorescent Tubes (circular or straight)
- Use the same cleaning method as for an incandescent bulb.
- NOTE: Manufacturers of fluorescent fixtures will differ in the way they construct a unit. If you do not have any experience in removing this type of tube lighting from its housing, and if you do not have an owner's manual to consult, call your local electric utilities service. Describe the tube's lighting design and ask how best to safely remove it for cleaning.

Light Diffusers, Shields (glass or plastic)
- Turn off the switch before cleaning. If possible, remove the part from the fixture or lamp.
- Wash in warm water and detergent. Rinse well and dry.

Lamps
- Lamp bases should be dusted routinely. Unlacquered wood and metal should be given a thin coat of paste wax. Glass, pottery, and marble bases can be wiped clean with a mild detergent and warm water. Always rinse well and buff dry with a soft cloth.

Lamp Shades

NONWASHABLE:
- Dry cleaning is the safest method. However, for a quick touch-up, remove the shade and dust with a soft brush, inside and outside. If it's easier for you, use the dusting tool of your vacuum cleaner.

WASHABLE FABRIC: To be "washable" means that the fabric must be sewn, not glued to the shade. Also, it should not have any glued-on trimming. If you do not

have the manufacturer's cleaning instructions and are not certain whether the shade is washable, try cleaning a small inconspicuous area inside the shade first.
- To clean, use lukewarm water and a light-duty detergent. Fill the sink or tub with enough of the washing solution so you can easily dip the shade up and down, rotating it to wash all areas. Rinse several times in fresh, clear, lukewarm rinse water to remove all traces of suds. Pat dry with an absorbent towel, then hang the shade outdoors in a shady spot if it's convenient, or use an indoor clothesline.
- Dry the shade as quickly as possible to avoid any chance of rust. If you plan to dry the shade indoors, use an electric fan to speed up the process.

WASHABLE PLASTIC:
- Wring a sponge out of warm water and wipe the shade inside and outside. To rinse, wring a fresh sponge out of clear warm water and wipe it repeatedly until all suds are removed. Dry with a fresh clean cloth.

Crystal Chandeliers
- First, turn off the light switch and let the bulbs cool before removing them.
- Hold the bulb by the end made of metal so you won't get it wet when washing. Wring a clean cloth out of warm, sudsy water to clean the bulb. To rinse, wring a fresh cloth out of clear, warm water. Dry well.
- To wash the crystal pieces, make a solution of several tablespoons of household ammonia to 1 quart of warm water. Take the solution, along with a clean soft cloth up the stepladder to the chandelier. Dip the

cloth in the solution. Squeeze water from the cloth until it is just damp, then wipe the crystal clean. Wipe dry with a paper towel.

Hanging Fixtures (track lighting and wall designs)
- Washable parts can be cleaned with mild detergent and warm water. The best way to clean each lighting piece is to follow the manufacturer's directions.

3. COOKWARE AND TABLEWARE

Modern cookware is made from many kinds of materials with an evergrowing choice of interior- and exterior-surface finishes. To clean your cookware properly, to maintain its appearance, and extend its useful life, take care to follow the manufacturer's recommendations on the label. Always read the instruction booklet carefully when you add a new pot or pan to your kitchen collection.

After use, wait for an excessively hot utensil to cool before washing it. A quick change from a very high temperature to a cooler one may harm the base of a range-surface pot, or cause damage to some types of ovenware casseroles (some glass or earthenware).

Dry all metal cookware carefully before putting them away. Some aluminum cookware can get dark-toned rings if stored while wet. Tin and cast iron may show signs of rust.

Cookware

Non-stick Finishes

Because of its easy-care surface, many users of non-stick finishes give it just a quick wipe with a paper towel; this is not proper care.

- To prevent a buildup of tiny particles of food and grease, wash the non-stick finish after each use in a mild soap or a light-duty detergent solution. Then rinse and dry it well.
- If you place your utensils in an automatic dishwasher, the strong detergent and high heat can rob them of some of their surface oils, and they will need to be reseasoned. (See instructions for seasoning under "Cast Iron" in this chapter.)
- Never use harsh metal scrubbers, steel wool, strong detergents, or abrasive scouring powders. To remove stubborn food spots or stains, use a nylon muff or mesh pad (safe for non-stick surfaces) and a very mild non-scratching cleanser that can be used on non-stick finishes, such as Bon Ami Deluxe Polishing Cleanser.
- After removing an unusually difficult stain, it may be a good idea to reseason the utensil's surface.

TYPES OF COOKWARE

Clean pots and pans according to the kind of material or materials of which they are made. Following are general care and cleaning suggestions for different metals and for glass cookware.

Aluminum Cookware
- To hand wash aluminum, use hot sudsy water; then rinse and dry. For burned-on food spots, soak the pan in hot suds for about 10 minutes; loosen the food spots with a soap-filled steel-wool pad; rinse and dry.
- On highly polished aluminum cookware, remove burned food by presoaking in hot suds; then use a nonabrasive nylon scrubber to remove the spots without marring the utensil's surface.
- For removing discolorations on aluminum, combine 2 tablespoons of lemon juice with 1 quart of water. Pour enough of this solution into the utensil to cover the stained portion. Simmer for about 10 minutes. (White vinegar may also be used in the proportion of ½ cup of vinegar to 1 quart of water.) Then rub the aluminum interior with a steel-wool soap pad. If the finish is polished aluminum, use a nonabrasive nylon scouring pad. Always work a cleaning pad in one direction around the utensil to avoid scratching it. Wash in hot suds; rinse well and dry.
- You can also eliminate stains and discolorations on aluminum cookware with a reliable commercial aluminum cleaner.

Cast-iron Cookware
Today most cast iron is given an oil-seasoning before it leaves the factory to keep it from rusting. If not, you can do it yourself according to the directions given below. (Also, check the manufacturer's label and instruction booklet.)
- Wash a new cast-iron utensil before using. Wash it by hand in hot sudsy water; rinse and dry it thoroughly.

If it has not already been seasoned, brush the interior surface with a thin coating of unsalted fat or vegetable oil. Remove wood handles and place the cookware in a very low oven for about 2 hours. (If handles are not removable, place the utensil on the range surface at the very lowest heat setting for about 30 minutes.) Remove the cookware from the heat and use a paper towel to wipe away excess seasoning oil. This will leave on just enough oil to protect the utensil.

- Clean cast iron as soon as possible after use so it will not rust from the moisture in foods. Don't soak cast-iron cookware and never use harsh scouring powders. Soften scorch or food spots by simmering 2 tablespoons of baking soda to 1 quart of warm water in the utensil for about 5 minutes. Use a soft brush to loosen the food spots. Then wash in hot suds; rinse and dry completely.
- Don't wash cast iron in a dishwasher if you want to avoid its possible rusting.
- If rust does occur, dampen very fine steel wool in warm water and rub the rust spot briskly. Another alternative is to use a mild scouring powder. In both cases, wash the utensil in hot suds, rinse well, and dry completely. Always follow up any rust removal by reseasoning.

Porcelain-coated Cast Iron: Some cast-iron cookware is coated with porcelain enamel on the interior and exterior but not on the base of the utensil. The porcelain glaze makes the utensil rust-resistant, but the non-glazed base must be cared for in the same way as uncoated cast-iron cookware. For care of the porcelain-coated cookware surfaces, see "Enamelware."

Copper Cookware
- Much of today's copper cookware is lined with either stainless steel or tin. Before using, follow the manufacturer's recommendations for removing the protective coating. Another suggestion is to submerge the utensil in intensely hot water until you are able to strip off the temporary exterior surface coating. (Some coating types melt off.)
- Wash all copper utensils on both the outside and inside in hot sudsy water. Rinse well and dry.
- Never use harsh abrasives on a copper surface. To remove stains, and also to polish copper, combine salt with either buttermilk, lemon juice, or white vinegar, in equal amounts. Dip a dampened cloth in this mixture and gently rub it over the copper surface.
- Another way to remove stains is with a reliable commercial cleaner made especially for copper. Apply according to the manufacturer's directions. Wash the copper surface well to remove residue; then rinse and dry.

Enamelware

Enameled cookware is made with a metal base such as steel, iron, or aluminum. However, in some cases, the exterior may be coated with another type of enamel finish. Due to these variations, it's best to read the labels on your cookware and follow the manufacturer's instruction booklet.

Enamelware is easy to clean, but is quite vulnerable to chipping, so use a light hand and caution.

- Let the cookware cool before cleaning it, as sudden changes in temperature may crack or craze the surface. Wash it in hot detergent suds; rinse and dry it well.

- Avoid using abrasive powders or steel-wool pads. Soak the utensil in a solution of 2 tablespoons of baking soda to 1 quart of warm water until the food spots have softened. Then, ease off the stains with a nonabrasive nylon-mesh scrubber pad; rinse and dry.
- Usually enamelware can be safely washed in an automatic dishwasher. However, do check your manufacturer's instruction booklet for precautions.

Glass and Glass-ceramic Cookware

Not all glass cookware can be used for top-of-the-range cooking, but it is cleaned in much the same way as oven-safe glass. Neither transparent glass nor opaque glass-ceramic cookware are affected by food acids, and neither type will rust. They are easily cleaned but will scratch, chip, or break if not cared for properly. Read labels, hangtags, and the manufacturer's instruction booklet for the most complete care and cleaning directions. Some additional cleaning suggestions are given here:

- Let glass cookware cool before washing. It is easily hand-washed with a light-duty detergent and hot water, but is safe in an automatic dishwasher. The one exception is decorated cookware that is rimmed with gold or silver. Metal trim will dull and begin to wear off from many dishwasher detergent washings.
- Never use harsh scouring powders or steel-wool pads. Avoid using metal stirring spoons or scrapers; these will mar the surface of glass-ceramic cookware. To remove these marks, dampen a plastic-mesh pad, dip it in either powdered whiting or baking soda, and rub this type of stain away.
- Soften burned-on food by soaking in a light-duty de-

tergent and hot water. Then ease the deposits off with a wood spoon or a nonabrasive plastic pad. To cut through greasy foods, add a few tablespoons of household ammonia to the detergent solution.
- For stains, soak the cookware in a solution of ½ cup liquid chlorine bleach to 1 quart of hot water. If necessary, use an exceptionally nonabrasive cleaner for very stubborn stains.
- NOTE: Check accessories, such as handles made of plastic, and remove them (unless the manufacturer directs otherwise) before putting cookware in the dishwasher.

Stainless-steel Cookware

Any item made of stainless steel is usually easy to clean, and will resist stains and rust. In cookware, stainless steel is generally combined with another metal; it may be used for the interior and exterior of a utensil, but the exterior base (or bottom) will be another metal such as aluminum or copper. Therefore, it is important to follow the manufacturer's cleaning instructions.

The care of other metals used in combination with stainless steel, such as aluminum and copper, appear elsewhere in this chapter, but general pointers on stainless-steel cookware are given here:
- Let a utensil cool before cleaning it. For handwashing, use a light-duty detergent and hot water; then rinse and dry with a soft towel. Some stainless steel will water-spot if left to air dry.
- The mirrorlike high polish on some stainless-steel cookware may be dulled by harsh dishwasher detergents. Check your owner's manual for the manufacturer's recommendations.

- Some foods that are high in acids or salts will cause dark markings on stainless steel. To avoid this, wash cookware as soon after use as possible.
- To remove the dull look caused by dishwasher detergents, use a good commercial cleaner and polish made especially for stainless steel. Use this same cleaner to remove dark markings on utensils caused by some dried-on foods.
- Never use harsh scouring powders or abrasive scouring pads. To remove burned-on food spots, first soak the utensil briefly, empty the water, and rub the stains with a dampened cloth dipped in baking soda. For more difficult food stains, make a paste by combining a very mild, *non-chlorinated* scouring powder with household ammonia and water. (Chlorine and ammonia should never be used together.) Use a plastic-mesh pad to rub the paste in one direction around the utensil's surface.

Tin Cookware

Utensils with a copper exterior often have an interlining of tin. Watch for the areas where the tin is worn out or wearing thin and have the utensil relined before you use it again. (See also "Copper" in this chapter.)

Check your owner's manual for special-care instructions for your tin or tin-lined cookware. Here are general suggestions for cleaning:

- Always let tin cookware cool before you wash it.
- Wash a tin utensil after each use in hot suds; rinse, and make sure it is thoroughly dried to avoid possible rust.
- To remove baked-on food spots, pour a baking-soda and hot-water solution (2 tablespoons of baking soda to 1 quart of water) into the tin utensil and let it sim-

mer over low heat for about 5 minutes. Pour off the liquid, and rub away the food stains with a rubber or nylon spatula. Wash the utensil in hot sudsy water, rinse, and dry.
- To remove rust spots from tin cookware, dip a cloth in cooking oil, then into an exceptionally mild, non-scratching cleaner such as Bon Ami Deluxe Polishing Cleanser. Rub the spot gently until it's gone. Wash the utensil, rinse, and dry thoroughly.

Cutlery

All knives need good care and should be treated the same way as your fine flatware.

Knife blades are made of carbon steel, stainless steel, or a combination of both called high-carbon stainless steel. Carbon-steel blades will hold a fine edge, but they stain easily from acids and are subject to rust. Stainless steel does not hold a sharp blade edge as well as carbon steel, but does resist stain and rust. High-carbon stainless steel combines the best characteristics of both its components.

Kitchen Knives

Be sure to read all labels that come with your knives and follow the recommendations of the manufacturer. Here are some general suggestions:
- Wash knives immediately after use. Don't let a knife soak in water; soaking can loosen the handle from the blade. Water will also warp a wood handle and cause the blade to rust.
- It's best to wash a sharp-edged knife by hand. *Handle*

with extreme care. Keep the sharp edge facing away from your hand in order to avoid being cut. Dip a sponge or cloth in hot suds and carefully wipe each knife individually. Rinse well and dry thoroughly.
- It is not necessary to use harsh scouring powders. Stains can usually be removed with a mild cleanser such as powdered whiting or baking soda sprinkled on the wet blade and rubbed with a dampened cloth.
- Generally, knives with wood handles should not be cleaned in a dishwasher. However, knives with handles made of moisture-resistant materials are claimed to be dishwasher-safe. If in doubt about the type of material, write to the manufacturer or inquire at a local retail store.

Tableware

Hand Dishwashing

Some fine tableware and dinnerware can be put in an automatic dishwasher; others are so fragile or valuable that hand-washing is preferable. Here are some items that must be washed only by hand:
- Antique china, usually the type that is hand-painted. For other lightweight, delicate china, frequently decorated with gold or platinum, it's a good idea to get the manufacturer's recommendations.
- Silver or silver-plate flatware with an antique finish.
- Antique milk glass.
- Knives that have bone, bamboo, wood, or hollow handles. Although manufacturers of modern hollow-handled knives claim that these are dishwasher-safe, it's wise to check with the individual maker.

- Wood utensils and bowls. (Items made of wood may warp or crack if kept in water for any length of time.)
- Pewter.
- Plastics. Some may be safe for dishwashers. Always look for the label or hangtag; it should state "dishwasher-safe."

As you wash the above items by hand, follow these basic pointers:

- Line the sink with several thicknesses of absorbent toweling or use a plastic dishpan. Never overcrowd the dishpan or sink. Use moderately hot water and a light-duty detergent for hand-washing. Protect your hands with moisture-proof gloves.
- Remove leftover foods and liquids from all dishes, glassware, and kitchen utensils. Quick rinse, or use a rubber or plastic scraper to remove leftovers on dishes in preparation for washing.
- Don't use abrasive cleaners, strong scouring powders, or steel-wool pads.
- To keep dishwater clean longer, wash in this order: glassware, metal tableware, china. These should all be washed before cookware. Rinse in clean, hot water.
- Air dry glassware and china on a dish rack and polish with a soft lint-free towel. Don't air dry metal tableware; buff it dry with a soft towel to prevent water spots. Towel dry all rust-prone utensils and equipment. Be sure all metal items are completely dry before putting them away.
- If it isn't convenient to wash metal tableware soon after use, at least rinse and dry it. Prolonged contact with acid or highly salted foods can discolor its surface.

Chinaware

Not only bone china and fine porcelain, but all types of dinnerware, including earthenware, stoneware, and plastic, are grouped under the name *chinaware*. While much of today's chinaware is safe in an automatic dishwasher, always check the china manufacturer's recommendations. Here are some general hints:

- Hand wash any metal-decorated or metal-trimmed china right after use if possible; rinse it to remove foods containing acids or lots of salt. Otherwise, these foods could dry on and mar its surface.
- Don't use a metal scraper; you might scratch the chinaware's surface. Use a rubber scraper for plates. Avoid the use of harsh abrasives or metal scourers.
- Hand wash fragile, antique, or hand-painted chinaware; also chinaware with platinum, gold, or silver decoration or trim.
- Don't use very hot water to wash or rinse this type of cookware. Extreme temperatures can craze or crack chinaware.
- Don't oversoak chinaware that has colored or metallic decoration over its glaze.
- The dark marks left by steel knife blades can be removed by gently rubbing them with a plastic-mesh pad and warm light-duty detergent suds.
- To remove a stain on plastic dinnerware, use a mild cleanser. Dip a damp cloth into some baking soda and rub the soiled area; then rinse and dry.
- Stains in coffee or tea cups can easily be removed from porcelain or informal china. Put ½ teaspoon of baking soda in the cup; then gently rub with a damp cloth.
- While melamine plastic is safe in automatic dishwashers, you should check any plastic that is un-

known to you for the statement "dishwasher-safe" on the underside, before placing it in the dishwasher. (See also "Hand Dishwashing" in this chapter.)

Glassware

Fragile, antique, hand-painted, or metal-rimmed glassware needs the special care of hand-washing. Here are some general hints:
- To wash long-stemmed, fragile goblets, hold each separately by its stem and slide it into the suds. Rinse each goblet before it has had time to cool. To drain, place the goblet, bowl opening downward, on a towel-covered flat surface. Dry with a soft, lint-free cloth.
- If glassware—antique, hand-decorated, or with its bowl rim outlined with platinum, silver, or gold—is given soakings, its decoration or trim could wear off.
- Hand-cut lead crystal should be washed with the same careful attention given your other elegant glassware. (See also "Glass and Crystal" in Chapter 5.)

Gold Plate

Gold-plated flatware varies in composition; it may be gold over sterling silver, gold over silver plate, or gold electroplate (gold over a durable base metal such as good-quality stainless steel).
- Keep gold-plated flatware free of any lengthy contact with highly acid or highly salted foods. Wash or rinse gold plate as soon as possible.
- In general, clean gold-plated flatware in much the same way you clean fine silver flatware. Most manufacturers recommend that you wash gold-plated flatware by hand, not in an automatic dishwasher. When hand-washing it, use only a mild light-duty detergent.
- When cleaning, don't press down heavily on the

metal with a strong scrubbing motion as this can wear away some of the gold.
- Never use harsh scouring powders.
- Give gold-plated flatware a gentle buffing with a soft dry cloth after it is washed and rinsed.

Pewter

Today's pewter flatware and serving pieces have a highly polished or a lustrous soft matte finish. Pewter is lead-free, usually tarnish-resistant, and under normal conditions is very easy to care for; check the manufacturer's recommendations. Some general cleaning tips are:
- Wash or rinse pewter as soon after use as possible to remove acid and salty foods.
- Most manufacturers recommend that you hand wash pewter in light-duty detergent suds and rinse well. If left to air dry, pewter may water spot, so use a soft cloth to buff it dry right away.
- Never use strong abrasive scouring powders or scratchy metal pads.
- Fine-quality modern pewter normally does not require polishing. To remove dullness or a dark mark, a cleaner or polish must be nonabrasive and made for pewter only.
- For the care of antique pewter, see "Pewter" in Chapter 5.

Silverware

Silver washes easily, either by hand or in an automatic dishwasher in hot water. Here is some general advice for cleaning sterling and silver plate:
- If moist salt or highly salted food remains on silver for any length of time, it can cause dark spots. Sul-

phur-containing foods, such as eggs and mayonnaise, and acidy foods will also tarnish silver. They should be washed off, or at least quick-rinsed, as soon as possible after a meal.
* Soaking silver can dull its finish.
* Treat flatware gently. Don't crowd an excessive amount in your dishpan or in the dishwasher's silver basket; one piece could scratch another.
* When using a dishwasher, keep silver from touching other metal pieces such as stainless steel or copper.
* Silver pieces with raised designs that have a darker shade in the crevices should always be washed by hand.
* Old or antique-finish silver should be hand-washed. Old silver knives with hollow handles cemented to their blades should be quickly hand-washed in water that is not too hot, or else the cement will soften and the handles will loosen.

Stainless Steel

This material is relatively easy to care for since it is nontarnishing and rust-resistant. However, the composition of the steel varies, and there are many different grades. Follow the manufacturer's advice for cleaning. Here are some general instructions:
* To prevent dark spots or streaks, wash or rinse off foods that are highly salted or very acid as soon as possible after each use.
* For hand-washing, use a light-duty detergent in hot water, rinse, and dry right away, or the stainless steel might water spot.
* If you are using an automatic dishwasher, keep stainless steel away from silver.

- Don't dull the bright surface of stainless steel with harsh cleaning powders and abrasive pads.
- To remove discolorations, use warm water and a nonabrasive cleaner such as powdered whiting or baking soda to form a soft paste. While your washed flatware is still damp, dip a dampened cloth into the paste and rub off the stains. Rewash, rinse, and dry.

Wood Tableware

Wood items such as salad bowls and servers, cheese trays, and serving trays can warp, crack, or develop small splinterlike grooves on the surface if not properly cared for. Simple ways to preserve wood items are:
- Clean wood pieces as soon as possible after use or, at least, discard leftover foods and use a paper towel to wipe off oils from salad bowls to prevent odors and possible stains.
- Wash each piece by hand, never in an automatic dishwasher. Use a light-duty detergent and warm water. Wipe each item thoroughly and quickly with a sudsy sponge and rinse at once in clear warm water. Dry completely.
- Avoid extremes in temperatures, such as inordinately cold or intensely hot water.
- Never soak wood in water, even briefly.
- To remove a stain, dampen a cloth and dip it in a very mild cleanser such as baking soda to rub away the stain. Odors from rancid oils in salad bowls can usually be removed by dipping a dampened cloth in lemon juice and wiping interior surfaces thoroughly. Rinse quickly and dry.
- Never use scouring powders or abrasive pads to clean wood.

4. FURNITURE

The appearance of even the simplest piece of furniture can be considerably enhanced by a clean, well-cared-for surface. Always save the manufacturer's booklet or tag that states the type of fabric or material, the finish, and any recommendations for cleaning.

TYPES OF FURNITURE

Wood Furniture
Wood furniture needs special care because too much moisture, dryness, or sunlight can cause it to blister, warp, or crack. Some basic suggestions for care are:
- Dust at least twice a week.
- Don't let water remain on the surface for any more time than it takes for a quick blotting-up. To avoid spreading a spill, use absorbent toweling.
- Keep furniture pieces away from windows that are frequently left open or from a strong heat source such as a radiator.

POLISHING:
- Polish wood furniture several times a year. Your choice of furniture polish should be guided by the finish rather than the type of wood. Furniture finishes range from high-gloss to semi-gloss to satin-gloss; there are polishes for each kind.

- Furniture polishes fall into two broad categories: those with an oil base and those that contain wax. Oil-based polishes give a dull sheen; wax polishes vary in the degree of shine. Remember, use only oil-type polishes on oiled finishes such as Danish teak. On antique furniture, always use paste wax.

CLEANING: When your furniture starts looking dull and smeared, or feels sticky, it's time to give it a thorough cleaning. You can use a commercial wood cleaner or this homemade one:

- Combine 1 part gum turpentine with 3 parts of boiled linseed oil. Saturate a fresh clean cloth and clean about a square foot at a time. Wipe it off with a second clean cloth right away, while the old wax and dirt is still moist. After cleaning, reapply the wax and buff to a shine.
- To remove white spots caused by water that was not quickly wiped off, get powdered rottenstone at a hardware store. Put a small amount on the spot and rub in lightly with a cloth dipped in lemon oil or mineral oil. Another idea is to combine cigarette ashes and soft butter. Put the butter on the end of a finger, dip in the ashes, and rub the spot gently with a circular motion. Then, remove the ash and butter mixture with a soft cloth.
- White alcohol marks can be treated with the same combination of ashes and butter used for water spots.
- Superficial scratches on dark wood can sometimes be hidden by rubbing with the meat of a walnut or Brazil nut or by touching it up with matching wax sticks, crayons, or brown shoe polish.
- Milk spills should be wiped up instantly and completely or white spots will show up the next time you

wax. If this happens, rub the spot briskly with a damp cloth, then rewax.
- To remove candle wax or chewing gum from your furniture, place ice cubes wrapped in plastic on top of the spot. Then lift off the hardened wax or gum with your fingers or use a dull knife to ease it off. Finish with an application of furniture polish.

Painted Wood Furniture

Wood pieces of furniture, often in bright colors for use in casual settings, need the type of paint that will withstand regular cleanings. In general, high-gloss enamel, an oil-based paint used on furniture, will hold up well under gentle washings. For routine cleaning:
- Dust furniture regularly.
- Wash, when necessary, in a solution of warm water and a light-duty detergent (the kind used for hand dishwashing and fine fabrics).
- Wash gently with a cloth or sponge dipped in the suds so as not to overwet the wood. Wash a small area at a time. Rinse thoroughly to remove all trace of suds. Dry with a soft cloth.

Upholstered Furniture

Fabric coverings stay fresh-looking longer and wear longer if you keep dirt and grit from settling and cutting into their fibers. Some basic instructions:
- Look for the manufacturer's label regarding the type of fabric and filling materials used (polyurethane foam, fiber fill, foam rubber, down feathers), and recommended cleaning methods. The label is usually found underneath a cushion. Also check hangtags.
- Be sure to blot up spills immediately, even if the fabric is stain-resistant.

- Use a good brush for frequent cleaning, at least once a week, or use the attachments from your vacuum cleaner. The upholstery tool will clean the larger areas, including the platform underneath cushions, both sides of the cushions, and over the back. The crevice tool will get into the corners and along the seams.
- NOTE: Don't use the vacuum cleaner on a down-filled cushion unless it is protected by an inner covering of durable ticking; the suction could pull out the down.
- When your upholstery needs a general, over-all cleaning, it's best to have a professional upholstery cleaner do the job.

LEATHER UPHOLSTERY:
- Wipe up spills at once with a damp cloth.
- To clean, dust first; then make suds by combining a mild pure soap with warm water. Wipe with only the lather and a damp cloth. Use a fresh cloth wrung out of clear, warm water and rinse repeatedly until every bit of suds is removed.
- To keep leather's pliancy, you may want to use a good commercial preservative. However, if the leather has been given a permanent finish, it needs no treatment or the finish will be ruined.
- When your leather (or suede) gets oversoiled or blemished, don't trust the cleaning project to just anyone; find a reliable, well-established professional repair service.

VINYL UPHOLSTERY: Flexible vinyl plastics can imitate leather so perfectly that you need to be sure which your furniture really is. Read the manufacturer's label, usually found under a cushion, for cleaning instruc-

tions. Since vinyls resist dirt and stains from acids, alcohol, food, and ink, cleaning is easy:
- Blot up spills right away.
- Clean by making a suds of either pure soap or a mild, light-duty detergent and warm water. Dampen a cloth or sponge in the suds and wipe. Rinse in clear warm water with a fresh cloth or sponge to remove all trace of suds. Wipe dry.
- Don't use harsh scouring cleaners or ammonia, acetone, or any type of cleaner that might contain a cleaning solvent.

Wicker/Rattan/Cane/Reed/Bamboo Furniture

This type of furniture often has a shellacked or painted finish which also protects it. In a natural finish, it not only can be subjected to water, but it actually requires moisture to keep from drying out.
- Dust furniture regularly. Use a clean cloth dampened in warm water. Or, use the dusting brush of your vacuum cleaner and the crevice tool attachment to draw out dust from all areas.
- Clean very soiled pieces by making suds with a mild soap or detergent and warm water, using a brush instead of a cloth to clean the furniture. It should not be soaking wet, however. Rinse with clear warm water. Dry well and quickly outdoors in a shaded area, or indoors using an electric fan.
- Don't let this type of furniture dry out or it will become brittle and eventually crack.
- On painted pieces, use water sparingly.

Wrought-iron Furniture
- Dust frequently.

- Wash with a brush dipped in a solution of light-duty detergent and warm water. Rinse and dry with a clean cloth.
- Protect from rust by periodically rubbing on a light coating of a good automobile wax.

Piano, Organ

The manufacturer will be able to provide you with the most complete answers to your questions about piano and organ care. Below are some general recommendations:
- Remove dust from the cabinet regularly. Today, most pianos and organs are lacquered and should not be polished.
- Wipe the keys with a clean, very soft cloth, or a soft chamois, lightly dampened in warm water. Use a fresh soft cloth to dry the keys thoroughly.
- Call a professional to check the instrument's inner workings and to clean the interior.

Stereo
- Clean the stereo cabinet and dust cover periodically with a soft dry cloth. For stubborn stains, use a cloth moistened with a mild detergent solution.
- As a general routine, the fabric portion of the speakers should be cleaned with the circular dusting tool of your vacuum cleaner. This will gently draw out accumulated dust.

Television
- Unplug the set before cleaning it.
- When cleaning the picture screen, use only a mild light-duty detergent and warm water. Wring a cloth

out of the suds so that it is just damp, and water will not seep into the set. Wipe the screen; then use another cloth wrung out of clear warm water to rinse. Dry and polish with a soft cloth.
- Use a good furniture polish on the wood cabinet but don't get any on the screen.
- Avoid having liquids anywhere near the set. If a spill occurs, blot it up right away. If you have even a slight suspicion that any water has gotten inside the set, call your television repair service at once. To be safe, don't use the set until it has been thoroughly checked.

SPECIAL FINISHES, SURFACES

Chrome
- Keep chrome gleaming by a daily dusting with a soft cloth.
- To remove any accumulated grime, wring a cloth out of hot suds and wipe the surface well. Rinse and polish dry.

Glass
- Wash glass-topped tables and glass bookshelves with warm water combined with a few tablespoons of white vinegar. Rinse and buff dry with a soft cloth or chamois. (See also Chapter 8, "Windows and Window Coverings.")

Marble Surfaces
When a marble tabletop shows slight signs of etchings and water marks that won't come off with a damp cloth, here is a method to remove these spots:
- Use a fine-grain oxide such as tin or aluminum (putty

powder). Mix the powder with a small amount of water to form a thin paste. Make a soft rubbing pad out of terry-cloth-type material. Dip the pad into the paste. Rub briskly. Keep the paste barely wet. As heat is generated, the paste will start to dry, consequently polishing the marble surface.
• When the stain is removed, ward off future etchings by applying a good protective dressing such as Italian Craftsman Polish to the surface. (See also Chapter 6, "Floors and Floor Coverings.")

Plastic/Plastic Laminate

As a general rule, plastic—in whatever form—is easy to care for. Here are some basic instructions for plastic finishes:
• Wipe up spills at once.
• Wash with a light-duty detergent in warm water, rinse, and dry with a soft cloth.
• Avoid using harsh scouring powders, abrasive cleaning pads, and strong bleaches. A stain will usually come off if you put some baking soda over it and rub with a dampened cloth.
• Use a cleaner-polisher made especially for laminates to give surface protection.

Plexiglas/Lucite

Furniture made of clear, rigid acrylic plastic is light and durable, but it scratches very easily.
• Use only cotton flannel cloths or absorbent cotton for cleaning.
• Dust with a damp cloth, then gently wipe dry.
• Wash, when necessary, in mild light-duty detergent suds. Or, if you prefer, use an ammonia-and-water solution. Rinse in warm, clear water.

- Never use a strong cleaner, scouring compounds, or any solvents.
- To protect the surface, when thoroughly clean, use a good grade of automobile paste wax.

5. DECORATIVE OBJECTS AND COLLECTIBLES

Whether you call them accessories, decorative objects, *objets d'art,* collectibles, or, maybe, room appointments—what you add to a room after its basic furnishings can make a total difference.

Some of these "objects"—whether sentimental, valuable, or simply useful and decorative—may need very little care; but all will need the right kind of care.

ACCESSORIES

Brass and Copper (e.g., bookends, candlesticks, fireplace accessories, vases, bowls, fireplace kettles, old tankards, mugs, watering cans)

Objects of brass and copper used only for display as room accessories are often given a lacquered finish during manufacture to keep the metals from tarnishing. Protect them against soil and moisture in order to make cleaning easier. To clean, here is all that's needed:

LACQUERED OBJECTS:
- Dust regularly with a soft cloth.
- To remove soil, wipe with a soft cloth. Wring out of lukewarm (never hot) water, and use a second cloth for drying.
- Keep a lacquered surface free from any type of cleaner-polish, whether commercial brands or homemade, as they will damage the finish.
- Remember that lacquered metals, especially copper, are reserved for display only and should never be used for cooking or serving food.

UNLACQUERED OBJECTS:
- There are effective commercial products made especially to clean unlacquered metal accessories. Some are labeled for an individual metal, such as brass; the label may also state that it can also clean copper and bronze. A product for cleaning copper *may* also clean stainless items. Read the manufacturer's directions on any cleaner-polish very carefully.
- Products marked "anti-tarnish" are designed to keep metals shiny for many months.
- Here's a suggestion for a homemade cleaner for unlacquered objects: use salt and a little white vinegar or lemon juice (just enough liquid to dissolve the salt). With a cloth, rub the tarnished item briskly, then rinse and polish it to a bright shine. (NOTE: For larger pieces, the proportion of 3–4 tablespoons of salt to 1 cup of white vinegar usually works very well.) If you make a paste by adding flour to the mixture, you will get a bright finish.
- For a softer look, combine a lightly abrasive powder such as rottenstone (available in hardware and paint

stores) with just enough salad oil to make a paste. Rub it well against the tarnish, wipe off the excess, and polish with a clean cloth. Another suggestion for a soft look is to combine powdered rottenstone with pure linseed oil.

Chrome (e.g., pitchers, picture frames)
* Wipe polished chrome with a damp cloth and polish dry.
* Wash with a cloth wrung out of warm suds to remove soil. Rinse and dry. Never use scouring powders; they will scratch the object's surface.

Glass, Crystal (e.g., old glass bottles, crystal decanters, milk-glass pitchers, vases)
* Remove the cloudy look from inside fine old bottles by filling them halfway with warm water, then adding a few tablespoons of household ammonia. Use a long, slim brush to get through a small neck opening; scrub the inside well. Remove the ammonia solution; wash in warm mild-detergent suds and rinse repeatedly until all traces of the ammonia and suds are removed. Use a soft cloth to dry and polish.
* To clean the intricate crevices on a cut-crystal decanter, use the tip of a cotton swab dipped in ammonia. Wash in a light detergent and warm water; then rinse with clear warm water plus a few tablespoons of white vinegar. Rinse thoroughly to remove the vinegar odor and all of the suds. Polish with a dry cloth.
* Wash milk-glass items singly in warm (not hot) water and mild detergent, then rinse in clear warm water.
* Don't use ammonia or harsh detergents on the sur-

face of glass pieces that are hand-painted or metal-trimmed, and don't let them soak in suds. (See also "Glassware" in Chapter 3.)

Gold, Gilt (e.g., frames for photographs, pictures, mirrors)
- Dust regularly with a soft dry cloth.
- If soil accumulates, or a spill is not wiped up and there is a stain, you need to know the kind of gold surface you have before trying to clean it. If it is pure gold, squeeze a cloth out of warm water until it's barely damp; then wipe away any hint of soil. Use a second cloth to polish it dry. But, it could also be gilded with a gold powder, a gold liquid, or gold leaf (defined as sheets of gold hammered to an extreme thinness); or it might be a combination of substitute materials designed to look like real gilt. A reliable picture-framing dealer will be able to tell you which kind of frame you have.

Leather (e.g., bookends, desk accessories)
- Keep such items free from dust. Leather preservatives are available that will help keep leather soft and pliable.
- To make your own leather dressing, combine 2 parts lanolin and 3 parts neat's-foot oil, first placing the lanolin in the top of a double boiler until it's melted. Add the neat's-foot oil. Stir until the mixture is blended. Add a small quantity of cedar oil, if you wish. Use a small amount at a time, and work it into the leather with a cloth. (This is suggested in the U.S. Department of Commerce publication "Care of Books, Documents, Prints and Films.")

Marble (e.g., ashtrays, art objects, small decorative boxes)
- Give decorative marble objects a regular dusting with a soft cloth. Use a damp cloth to wipe away soil. Polish dry.
- Remove spills right away; then make suds of a mild detergent and water to wash the area. Rinse with clear warm water. For information on stain removal, see "Marble Surfaces" in Chapter 4.

Mirrors
- Be especially careful not to use too much cleaning solution; it could run down into the mirror's backing and damage it.
- Abrasive cleansers are harmful to mirrors. A mild but effective homemade solution is: 2 tablespoons of household ammonia to 2 quarts of warm water; or, use 2–4 tablespoons of white vinegar to 2 quarts of warm water.
- If you are using a spray, aim it first on a lint-free cloth to avoid dripping. Clean only one workable area of the mirror at a time; then wipe immediately with a clean cloth. Repeat for all other areas of the mirror. To eliminate streaks, polish the mirror with a chamois.

FRAME PROTECTION: The mirror's frame also needs protection from excess cleaning solution.
- Place a piece of heavy cardboard against the inside edge of the frame. If the frame is unavoidably splashed with cleaning solution, wipe it off at once with a dry cloth. After the mirror is cleaned, wipe the entire frame with a cloth wrung out of warm water. Dry it completely with a fresh clean cloth. You may wax the frame, if you wish.

Pewter (e.g., antique candlesticks, pitchers, tankards, mugs)
- Wipe off dust regularly; get rid of soil caused by handling by wiping the objects with a damp cloth, followed by a gentle rubbing with another dry cloth. When any pewter object looks a bit dulled from an accumulation of air pollutants and soil, wash it in a light-duty detergent and warm water. Never use abrasive powders or all-purpose detergents. Always rinse in clear water and dry well.
- NOTE: To wash some pewter pieces, such as an old tankard with a wood handle or a wood base, don't immerse it in water. Squeeze a cloth out of light-duty detergent suds and wash the metal only, rinse, and dry; then wipe the wood parts with a cloth wrung out of clear water, and dry thoroughly. Wax the wood, if you wish.
- Loosen candle wax in a pewter candleholder by holding it under warm running water. Ease out the softened wax with a soft cloth; then wash, rinse, and dry the candleholder.
- Use a good, established brand of pewter polish to remove dark marks or stains when they occur. Follow directions for polishing and cleaning, printed on the polish's container. Afterward, wash, rinse, and dry the surface. (See also "Pewter" in Chapter 3.)

Plexiglas/Lucite/Rigid Acrylic Plastic (e.g., small accessories, frames for desk photographs, paperweights)
- Dust regularly with an especially soft cloth; the highly polished surface of see-through acrylic plastic tends to scratch easily.

- Don't use strong abrasive cleaners. Avoid strong solvents, especially alcohol and acetone (present in nail-polish remover).
- Wash, when necessary, in a light-duty detergent and warm water. Household ammonia in water is also recommended. Rinse in clear warm water. Use a soft cloth to dry and polish the surface. A periodic waxing with a hard automobile paste wax like Simonize (not a cleaner-wax combination) will fill in minor scratches and restore luster. Apply wax sparingly and buff lightly with absorbent cotton or cotton flannel. (See also "Plexiglas/Lucite" in Chapter 4.)

Porcelain (e.g., hand-painted eggs, delicate figurines, hand-decorated plates, vases, cups and saucers, antiques)
- Hand-washing is recommended. Avoid harsh detergents and scouring powders.
- Use a light-duty detergent in warm water to wash. Rinse in clear water and dry at once.
- Wash delicate figurines and rare old plates individually. Figurines may easily chip; plates, when wet, should not be allowed to slide against each other.
- Don't soak decorated or metal-trimmed china. (See also "Chinaware" in Chapter 3.)

Pottery, Earthenware
- Use warm water with a light-duty detergent to wash. Rinse in clear warm water and dry with an absorbent towel.
- Don't run the risk of chipping by overcrowding in the sink.
- Don't oversoak in suds.

Silver (e.g., candlesticks, flower bowls, vases and old urns, coffee/tea service, large beverage pitchers, trays)

LACQUERED DISPLAY SILVER:
- Keep free of dust as a regular routine. Use a soft clean cloth (not starched).
- Squeeze a cloth out of warm (not hot) water to wipe away any collected soil. Dry by polishing with a second soft cloth.
- NOTE: Silver pieces that are used for serving food should never be lacquered.

UNLACQUERED DISPLAY SILVER:
- An anti-tarnish silver polish will keep a coffee or tea service, beverage pitchers, and trays clean and gleaming for months.
- Wear plastic rather than rubber gloves when polishing silver.
- NOTE: After polishing *any* silver item, wash off all traces of the polish. Use a light-duty detergent in warm water; rinse in clean warm water and buff dry with a soft cloth.

SILVER-AND-WOOD COMBINATIONS:
- Avoid overwetting or soaking these combinations, such as a coffee pot with a wood handle.
- Don't plunge these items into suds. Wring a cloth out of the wash water and wipe the silver surface only. Use clear water to rinse; then dry. Wipe the wood handle with a dampened cloth wrung out of clean water. Dry it thoroughly and wax it lightly if you wish.
- NOTE: To avoid fruit acids on silver, add a glass insert to a tray or bowl used to hold fresh fruit. (See also "Silverware" in Chapter 3.)

Wood (e.g., carvings, accessories)
- Dust regularly to prevent gritty soil from settling and scratching the surface finish. Blot up spills at once. Water left on wood for a period of time can cause staining, warping, and even splitting.
- In general, it is safe to clean and protect such items with a good paste wax, several times a year. However, you should consider the finish of your particular wood display piece before proceeding. (See also "Wood Furniture" in Chapter 4 and "Wood Tableware" in Chapter 3.)

ARTWORK

In the care and cleaning of valuable artwork, it is far more practical to trust the job to a professional than try to do it yourself. Experts who spend most of their lives studying and working in this highly specialized field can make judgments and recommendations that are worth the expense.

The initials AIC represent an organization made up of certified conservators based in Washington, D.C. If you wish to contact them, specify whether you are particularly interested in the conservation of picture frames, furniture, paintings, sculpture, fine minerals, or paper. Ask for a listing of certified conservators in your area. The full name and address of AIC is: The American Institute for Conservation of Historic and Artistic Works, Suite 804, 1522 K Street, N.W., Washington, D.C. 20005.

Pictures
Whether it's an oil painting, a watercolor, a graphic art print, or a photograph, one place to begin asking

questions about its handling and care is your local museum of fine arts. In a large city it may be necessary to contact someone in a specific museum department, such as painting conservation, if you are concerned about an oil painting, for example, and wish to find a qualified restorer. Or, if need be, check the Yellow Pages to find one. If you plan to take your artwork to the studio of a restorer with whom you aren't familiar and ask for an opinion of your artwork's condition, inquire about the fee and also for references.

One museum curator explains the reason for extreme caution this way: "Only an expert can assess an oil painting's state of preservation. He will know if the paint is well attached. It could be loose, and a layman would not realize it. In this case, it could be a risk to even dust it."

GLASS-COVERED PICTURES:
- Clean the glass in the same manner suggested for cleaning a mirror. Be careful not to let any moisture get under the frame and onto the picture.

Sculpture
- Keep bronze and marble dusted. When soil collects, wipe it with a cloth dampened in lukewarm water. Buff dry with a fresh cloth.
- The home cleaners for unlacquered brass and copper will also clean unlacquered bronze. However, if you have difficulty removing stains and excessive tarnish on a prized piece of bronze, consult a professional restorer to assess its true condition.
- Do not use any type of cleaner-polish, either commercially made or otherwise, on bronze that has been

patinaed or lacquered. Wipe up spills right away, and if any damage should ever occur, don't try to remedy it yourself; consult an expert regarding its repair.

FABRIC AND FIBER CRAFTS

For care and stain-removal suggestions not covered in this section, see "Upholstered Furniture" in Chapter 4, and "Stain Removal" in Chapter 9.

Small Rugs

Today you'll find that small contemporary or oriental rugs are hung on the wall as artwork.
- To keep colors looking fresh, dust regularly. Take the hanging down from the wall, lay it on a flat surface, and vacuum. Depending upon its size and weight, you'll know whether it's easier to use the dusting tool attachment or your regular vacuum attachment to do the cleaning. (See also "Carpets" in Chapter 6.)

Tapestry and Needlepoint Panels
- To dust, remove the hanging from the wall and place it on a smooth, flat surface. Treat it with care. Use the dusting tool of the vacuum to clean, but hold it well above the embroidery to avoid any possible contact. This should draw out the dust without harming the design.

Framed Fabrics
- Retain any manufacturer's hangtags describing how to care for and clean hand-print fabrics. They will be easier to keep clean if they have been chemically

treated to resist soil, stains, and moisture. Dust them regularly, as well as their frames, with the dusting brush of the vacuum cleaner.

Decorative Pillows
- Before cleaning, read the manufacturer's tag to learn if the pillow has been chemically treated to resist soil and stains.
- If hand-worked yarns or threads are part of your pillow's decorative design pattern, they may not withstand the strong suction of a vacuum cleaner's dusting brush. Hold the dusting attachment well above the surface of the fabric to avoid damage; or use a very soft hand brush to dust with care.

BOOKS

- Dust regularly with a soft cloth, a soft flexible brush, or the dusting brush of the vacuum cleaner.
- Close a book before dusting it. Hold the book tightly together in an upright position.
- Clean book edges that look grimy in this way: rub an art gum eraser gently over the edge of the pages. Use a soft brush to dust off the eraser's "crumbs."
- Brush the book's entire surface with the vacuum's dusting tool.
- You'll find good, commercially made leather-cleaning compounds at reliable book-binding stores. To make your own, this lanolin and neat's-foot oil combination is suggested in the U. S. Department of Commerce's "Care of Books, Documents, Prints and Films": To combine two parts lanolin and three parts neat's-

foot oil, first place lanolin in the top of a double boiler until it's melted. Add the neat's-foot oil. Stir until the mixture is blended. Add a small quantity of cedar oil if you wish. Use a small amount at a time, and work it into the leather cover with a cloth.

6. FLOORS AND FLOOR COVERINGS

In order to clean and care for your floors and carpets properly, you should know their characteristics. Finding out about the type of material your floors or carpeting is made of will go a long way to protect it against the ravages of use and time.

Types of Floors

Brick Floors
Today's floor bricks are often glazed, resistant to stains, and therefore relatively easy to clean. Unglazed bricks can be given a long-lasting sealer finish as an added protection against soil. General care suggestions are:
- To remove daily dust, sweep or vacuum. Damp mop to keep the floor looking fresh.
- Wash, when soil accumulates, in a solution made by adding ½ cup washing soda to 1 gallon of warm water. Rinse thoroughly in clear warm water.

Cork Floors

Cork, like wood, is porous and needs a sealer finish and a wax coating to protect it from the effects of water, excessive soil, and heavy foot traffic. While some cork floors are sealed at the factory, for others it is necessary to apply the sealer yourself. Ask a reputable flooring retailer about your particular type of floor and for a manufacturer's instruction booklet.

- In general, a cork floor is cared for just like a wood floor. When a wax is needed for general upkeep, it should be one with a solvent base. (See also "Wood Floors" in this chapter.)

Marble Floors

Marble is both beautiful and practical. Routine maintenance can be quite easy. Here are some basics:
- Remove dust and light soil by damp-mopping as a regular routine.
- Use a light-duty detergent (the type used for handwashing fine fabrics) plus a small amount of ammonia to wash the floor when more than a casual damp-mopping is necessary. Rinse thoroughly in clear warm water. Eliminate all traces of the detergent so it cannot seep into the porous marble. Dry completely and buff.
- NOTE: Do not use soap, as it can leave a film or residue that will attract dirt. Also, don't use abrasive cleansers on polished marble floors, as they can dull the surface and scratch it.
- Protect the floor by wiping spills right away, *especially* any acid-type foods, citrus juices, and carbonated drinks. These spills can eat through the surface polish and damage the marble.
- For a specific type of stain, consult a professional

marble dealer or a retail marble-supply firm. Be prepared to describe the stain, its cause, and when it occurred.
- After wiping up spills such as coffee, tea, some cosmetics, or tobacco, usually these discolorations can be removed with a combination of 3 percent hydrogen peroxide and a few drops of ammonia. First, put together two or three thicknesses of absorbent paper toweling or cloth; dip it into the peroxide solution, place it over the stain, and cover it with plastic wrap to keep the moisture in. It may take several hours, depending upon the stain. You may need to repeat the procedure if it doesn't work the first time.
- For a discoloring stain caused by grease or oily food, dip some paper toweling or cloth into a nonflammable dry-cleaning fluid. Place the saturated cloth over the stain and cover with plastic wrap. Keep the room well-ventilated, and keep children and pets away from the area.
- To remove tiny scratches or light superficial etchings, get the finest grade of sanding paper from a retail marble-supply dealer. This paper is often black, with an exceptionally fine mesh. Cut a piece of sanding paper to a comfortable working size and then sand the etching gently. Next, mix polishing putty powder (tin oxide) with just enough water to form a paste that is barely wet and briskly rub it on the etching with a soft cloth. As the rubbing continues, the paste will dry a bit; heat will be generated; and the etching should disappear. This takes patience. Thoroughly rinse the stained area with water and dry it well. (Some possible sources to buy putty powder are hardware stores, chemical-supply stores or stone dealers.)
- Finish up any stain- or etching-removal procedure by

buffing the area by hand or with an electric polisher.
- To remove any large, severe etchings, it is most practical and safest to entrust the project to a reliable marble polisher who has the necessary special equipment for the job.

Slate Floors
- Clean slate floors in much the same way as marble, even though slate is somewhat rougher.
- Routinely damp mop the floor. When necessary, use a light-duty detergent in warm water to wash the floor. Do not use soap, which can dull the slate. Rinse well and dry. For further cleaning details, see "Marble Floors" in this chapter.
- NOTE: According to the Building Stone Institute, waxing slate is not harmful, but it detracts from the natural beauty of this stone and may turn the color of the floor to a darker shade. It may also yellow the grout.

Terrazzo Floors
Give this superior flooring the same care you give to a marble floor. Terrazzo floors are made of crushed marble chips and can be polished to have the silky-smooth sheen of marble. Follow the suggested care routine for marble floors since this type of flooring is composed of more marble than cement.

Tile Floors (Ceramic)
The most popular flooring for bathrooms, ceramic tiles in innovative designs are now being used in other areas of the home as well. Some general care suggestions are:

- Wipe up spills at once, especially paint or medicine. It usually is not necessary to do more than damp mop as a regular routine.
- Wash the floor, when necessary, in warm water to which you've added some washing soda. This will remove most spots and stains from the tile. To rinse, use clear warm water.
- With a nonabrasive cleanser, scrub areas where greasy grime may have accumulated over a period of time. Rinse thoroughly in warm water.
- NOTE: When time is limited and there are difficult stains to remove, such as dried-on paint or rust, there are effective commercial products available at paint and hardware stores to do the job.

Tile Floors (Quarry)

This colorful, durable, hard-duty floor tile will stand up to heavy foot traffic.
- Keep quarry tile floors dusted. Damp mop, when necessary.

Vinyl Floors

The most resilient flooring manufactured in the United States today is vinyl. It is even more popular than linoleum, which is not waterproof. Vinyl flooring is resistant to greasy dirt and most scuffs and stains. In some cases it has the advantage of a no-wax surface. Here are some suggestions on floor care:
- Even a durable surface can be damaged when gritty soil is not removed. In a busy household it's usually necessary to sweep or vacuum the floor every day.
- Wash the floor when it starts to look a bit colorless and worn from an overall blanket of grime. First sweep or vacuum off the surface dirt. Then mix a

general-purpose liquid detergent, not a harsh one, with warm water. Moisten a small area with a mop and let the cleaning solution soak into the surface for a minute or so. Then use a scrubbing motion to pick up any stuck-on dirt. Wring out the mop and wipe up the area. Use another mop to rinse thoroughly with clean water from a second bucket. (Keep a second mop to use only for rinsing.) Continue to wash and rinse until the entire floor is washed. Change the rinse water whenever it begins to look dirty.

WAXING FLOORS:
- Wax the floor when it loses its lively gloss. Use a water-based wax made for resilient floor coverings. Some of the waxes give a soft, satiny look and require buffing. Others clean and polish all in one application. Most water-based waxes are self-polishing. Whichever you choose, follow the manufacturer's directions.
- Although instructions on how to wax floors vary from one product to another, here's a general procedure: Begin with a clean floor. Use wax sparingly. Spread the wax on evenly over a small area at a time. Let the floor dry completely before walking on it (usually about a half hour).
- Remove the many coats of wax about once a year. The sparkling shine of your vinyl floor can become dull and dingy after six or eight coats of wax have been added, one over the other.

WAX REMOVAL:
- Remove as much dirt from the floor as possible before sweeping or vacuuming it.
- Although there are many good wax-removing products on the market, here's a solution you can prepare

yourself. Mix 1 cup of ammonia with ¼ cup of powdered floor cleaner plus ½ gallon of cool water.
- Dip a hand sponge, cloth, or sponge mop in the wax or polish-removing solution of your choice. Generously wet a floor space of about three feet square. Let the stripping solution sink into the old layers of wax or polish to soften the built-up film. Usually this takes 3 to 5 minutes.
- Use a nonabrasive nylon floor-scouring pad to loosen any dirt and the built-up film of old wax. An electric floor scrubber can be a convenience. Check to be sure it has pads that will scrub, not scratch, the floor.
- With a sponge mop or a cloth, mop up the solution, dirt, and loosened wax or polish.
- Rinse thoroughly with a clean sponge mop and clear rinse water until there is no dirt or bits of waxy residue left.
- Repeat the above procedure one part of the floor at a time. If any area still has any built-up film, use a dull-edged spatula to gently scrape across it, and then repeat the above cleansing method.
- Give the floor time to dry thoroughly before walking on it.
- Put on a new coat of polish, following the manufacturer's directions for the water-based product you use.

NO-WAX SURFACES: These surfaces give a gleaming shine that will not need waxing or buffing far longer than uncoated vinyl. Dirt, spills, and even black heel marks can be removed more easily.
- Sweep or vacuum regularly no-wax vinyl floors.
- Sponge mop when necessary and always rinse thoroughly. This is the only restorative needed to keep your floor shining. Eventually, the shine may have to

be touched up with a special finish available at most hardware stores.

Wood Floors

When a wood floor is in good condition and the surface has a reliable finish, its care is relatively simple.
- Go over a wood floor with a soft lint-free dry dust mop; or use the "floor" attachment of a vacuum cleaner to remove dust and gritty soil brought in from outdoors. This may be done daily, weekly, or even less often, depending upon how much use the floor gets.
- In case of a liquid or food spill, wipe it up immediately with a clean, absorbent cloth.
- To remove a stain, use extra-fine-grade steel wool. Dip it in paste wax, rub the stain gently in the direction of the wood grain; then rewax the stained area.
- Keep water away from wood floors. Water left on wood (or cork) can damage the finish. In addition, when moisture comes in contact with the wood, it can stain, raise the grain, and even cause the wood to become swollen or warped.
- Protect the floor's finish with a good wax. Some floors may need waxing two or even three times a year.
- If wax has worn off in front of an entranceway or any area that gets a lot of wear, you can spot wax. These small touch ups can delay the need for overall waxing.
- Any hard, sharp objects, such as nails, left lying around can damage your floor's surface. Also, be careful when moving heavy furniture, such as chairs with pointed legs, to put protection under the legs,

and pads under heavy desks or other pieces of furniture, so as not to gouge or scratch the floor's finish.

SOLVENT-BASED WAX: Waxes meant for wood or cork floors are solvent-based; they contain no water. Check the wax's label to be sure it's designed especially for wood floors, and to follow the manufacturer's directions for its use. *Never* use a water-based wax on wood. Solvent-based waxes come in paste or liquid form. These can require buffing or be self-polishing.

- Before waxing, see that your floor is clean and completely dry.
- Wear comfortable gloves to protect your hands; and, don't smoke. The room should be well ventilated.
- Work on a small area at a time. With a clean cloth or a wax applicator, spread the wax thinly and evenly. (Don't use a sponge or a sponge mop, as the solvent could cause it to disintegrate.) Replace the cloth or applicator pad when it becomes soiled, and keep it well-moistened with wax. Work one small area at a time, until the entire floor is waxed.
- Make sure the floor is thoroughly dry before buffing it.
- Never store the soiled, solvent-soaked materials used in waxing until they are washed clean and dried. (See also "Wax Applicator Pads" in Chapter 1.)

FLOOR-WAXING MACHINES: An electric floor-waxing machine designed for home use may be rented. Make sure that it operates on the current used in your home and follow the manufacturer's directions for proper operation.

WOOD-FLOOR REFINISHING: If your floor is worn and

old-looking, has experienced water damage, or is severely scratched, it will need refinishing.
- Remove all traces of the old finish, sand the floor, sweep it thoroughly, then apply a sealer. It is wise to entrust this job to a well-recommended floor-care professional.

Carpets and Rugs

By giving your carpets and rugs daily attention they will look and wear better for a longer time. On a day-to-day basis, all that may be needed is a few strokes with a carpet sweeper. It is especially important to pay immediate attention to removing spills so they won't become permanent stains on your carpet or rug. (See also Chapter 9, "Stain Removal.")

Each week, use your vacuum cleaner for a more thorough cleaning job. When necessary, perhaps every year or so, an in-depth major cleaning may be needed, when the fresh colors in your carpet and rugs take on a dulled, drab look. With time, fibers become covered with greasy soot that weekly vacuuming does not remove.

For do-it-yourselfers there are stores that sell or rent carpet-cleaning equipment and supplies. Find out about available cleaning products and equipment made for wet- and dry-cleaning methods. Whichever system, product, or equipment you use, carefully following the manufacturer's instructions will bring the best results.

Some basics to clean your floor coverings are:
- Vacuum rugs on both sides before a more thorough cleaning.

- Before using a cleaning solution, test it on an inconspicuous area of the carpet to see its effect on carpet dyes.
- Take special care not to overwet carpeting.

HOME CARPET CLEANING

DRY METHOD:
- An absorbent cleaning compound is brushed in and around the carpet fibers. It may be done by hand, but special machines for this type of cleaning are more efficient. Embedded soil, oil, and grease is absorbed by the compound, then removed by vacuuming. Generally, this method is most effective in removing soil with a high oil and grease content; and it usually produces a good finish or appearance. On a heavily soiled carpet, it may not remove as much dirt as some other methods.

WET METHOD:
- This is a good system if you carefully follow the directions for the correct dilution and application of the cleaning detergent in order to avoid overwetting the carpet; protect your furniture during the cleaning; and use quick and thorough drying techniques. (See "Hot-water Extraction" on the following page.)

FOAM SPRAY:
- Each foam spray on the market has its own specific directions for you to follow. Aerosols produce a dry foam, as do some of the liquid preparations that are to be mixed with water.
- Because this system uses a minimum of water, it's not likely to overwet the carpet. Although it is just surface cleaning, the foam-spray method, if used prop-

erly, will improve the looks of your carpet. On an overly soiled carpet, the system is not very effective.

HOT-WATER EXTRACTION:
- Special equipment must be rented for this method, sometimes called "steam cleaning." A cleaning solution is forced into the pile of the carpet at high pressure. Deeply embedded soil and a large amount of the solution are immediately vacuumed out. Because a large volume of water is used in this system, it's important to carefully follow the manufacturer's directions to avoid overwetting the carpet.

UNDERPADDING:
- Vacuum the separate padding for your carpets and rugs every six months or so. Check it carefully to see if it needs repair.

Ways to Manage Mildew

Although carpets and rugs made today are mildew-resistant, dampness and greasy soil encourage mildew growth.
- Don't skimp on your vacuuming schedule.
- Remove spills at once.
- Don't overwet your carpet or rugs.
- Dry any wetness quickly and thoroughly.
- Take rugs outdoors, if possible, to brush any mildewed areas so you won't have mildew spores in the house. Expose the mildew to the sun for several hours, then vacuum thoroughly. If you use the upholstery attachment to remove the mold, discard the disposable vacuum bag at once. If you're uncertain whether all mold has been removed, call a professional carpet cleaner.

TYPES OF CARPETING AND RUGS

Cotton Carpeting
- Cotton is inclined to mat down when it's wet and takes quite a while to dry thoroughly. Cotton is susceptible to mildew; it must always be completely dried. Therefore, when your wall-to-wall carpet is in need of overall cleaning, it's wise to have a professional cleaner do the job to make certain that, along with the soil, the cleaning solution residue is removed from the cotton fibers.

Outdoor Carpeting
Outdoor carpeting is generally well constructed of sturdy man-made fibers that are resistant to both weather and stains. The backing is also weather-resistant to ward off mildew and rot.
- To remove gritty dirt, sweep or hose the carpeting occasionally. Refer to the manufacturer's directions for specific care and use.

Coarsely Woven Rugs
Because of their rather loose weave, these rugs should generally not be put in an area that gets heavy foot traffic.
- Since many coarsely woven rugs are made with blends of more than one fiber, follow the manufacturer's directions for routine cleaning. After vacuuming these rugs, roll them up and clean the floor since dirt may have seeped through the rug; then clean the reverse side of the rug.
- For major cleaning, have a professional do the job.

Handmade Braided or Hooked Rugs

The safest method is to have a professional cleaner attend to these types of rugs. Rinsing all the cleaning solution out of these rugs without overwetting them is a difficult job. Also, you cannot hang such rugs over a clothesline to dry without straining the stitches or loosening the loops. A few suggestions are:

- Roll up the rug when sending it out to be cleaned. Don't bend or fold it.
- Clean these rugs before you store them (in a rolled-up fashion).
- Don't shake or beat the rugs to remove dust; don't put them in a washing machine; and always handle them with care.

Oriental Rugs

The important points about cleaning these hand-woven, hand-knotted, elegant rugs made in the Orient are:

- When you purchase oriental rugs, file away for future reference the fiber content, country of origin, and its manufacturer's name and/or the brand name of the pattern and color. This is important information when you need advice about a cleaning or repair problem.
- As with other rugs, give oriental rugs a light cleaning every day with a carpet sweeper and a thorough vacuuming every week. Make sure that all spots or spills are removed at once. In addition, give them a periodic major cleaning by a specialist in oriental rugs. According to the amount of use it gets, this could be once a year; or where there is light activity, every two or three years.
- Even small oriental rugs should not be washed at home.

- As for the type of care you should expect when a specialist supervises a cleaning project, one expert says: "Your rug must be examined before and after cleaning and prespotted, if necessary. You should be informed if there are any moth-eaten areas, burns, frayed edges or fringes, or fallen knots."
- Roll up your rugs when storing them. Never fold them when you send them out to be cleaned.

Shag Rugs
- When vacuuming, try not to fray the long, luxuriant yarns in a shag rug. Some upright vacuum cleaners have a special shag height adjustment or a shag attachment. If your vacuum has neither, turn it to its highest setting. To raise some of the rug's tufts that fall or mat down, use a shag rake to comb through them. (Shag rakes are usually found in department stores.)
- When a deep shag rug needs a major cleaning, call a professional carpet cleaner.

7. WALLS AND CEILINGS

Regular cleanups—dusting, removing spots as soon as possible, frequent washing of most-likely-to-soil areas—all delay the day when a general cleaning becomes an urgent necessity. This is true whether your walls are painted, paneled, covered with non-washable or washable wall coverings or ceramic tile. Here is a plan of action for a major cleanup of your walls and ceilings:

- Take down pictures, mirrors, and other wall hangings. Cover books and lighting fixtures with plastic wrap. Remove area rugs. Cover wall-to-wall carpeting and vinyl-covered or wood floors. (If you move your furniture to the center of the room, the walls will be more accessible.) Cover all furniture with sheets of plastic. You might schedule this overall cleanup when your curtains and draperies are away at the cleaner.
- Wrap a clean cloth around a broom or long-handled dust mop in order to dust off all ceiling areas. If convenient, you might prefer using the dusting brush of the vacuum cleaner.
- Dust the walls after you have finished with the ceiling; when dusting, begin at the top of the wall and work down. Don't forget to dust the woodwork.

Painted Walls and Ceilings
- If you are not certain whether the paint is washable, test a small area with the cleaning solution you plan to use.
- Good commercially made products designed for painted surfaces include foam cleaners and powdered wall cleaners that are combined with water. Here is one homemade cleaning solution: To 1 gallon of warm water, add 1 cup of non-sudsy household ammonia, ½ cup of white vinegar, and about 3 tablespoons of baking soda.
- Don't use abrasive scouring powders or cleaners; they may fade or wear off the paint.
- As a general rule, don't scrub to remove grime; use a gentle washing motion.
- Wash walls from the bottom up; work one small area at a time.

WOODWORK, BASEBOARDS, WINDOW AND DOOR FRAMES:
- If you don't know the type of paint used, test a small surface area to see if it's washable. Enamel or high-gloss paints can usually withstand stronger washing.

Paneling
- Never use strong abrasive cleaners or steel wool on any type of paneling.
- To get the soil out of wood paneling or natural-finish woodwork, clean with liquid wax and rub to a soft polish. Read the label on any cleaning polish you want to try, to make sure it is exactly right for your type of wall paneling.
- Don't use water on wood surfaces.
- If a scratch on your paneling is only superficial, it will often disappear if you use a coating of good clear

paste wax, rubbing with the grain. However, if the scratch is deeper, commercially made sticks and other products may be useful. When a scratch has broken through the surface finish into the wood, it's best to consult a professional refinisher. (See also "Wood Furniture" in Chapter 4.)
- Walls made of Formica or other plastic laminates should be cleaned with an all-purpose spray or liquid cleaner and buff-dried. Stubborn stains can be treated with a porcelain cleaner; never with abrasives or steel wool.

Papered Walls

NON-WASHABLE WALL COVERINGS: These wall coverings are usually elegant and often expensive screen or hand prints.
- Use a soft brush to remove loose soil and dirt during regular dusting.
- Be quick to eliminate spots that, if left to "set" on the wallpaper, may become stains.
- To clean, use a dough-like cleaner product, generally found at paint and wall-coverings stores. Do not use water or water-based products to clean. Read carefully the manufacturer's instructions before starting to clean the wall coverings.
- If you have a stain problem on a particularly delicate wallpaper, it's wise to consult a reputable wall-coverings dealer for the safest cleaner to use.

WASHABLE WALL COVERINGS: Not all wall coverings that are water-resistant are also washable. Because there are so many types of coverings in the water-resistant category, it's best to make a test first. Wet a sponge in sudsy water and test the covering in an in-

conspicuous place. Here are some other suggestions:
- To remove dirt and soil, a damp cloth is usually sufficient. Avoid using abrasive scouring powders and steel wool. When necessary, use a light-duty detergent in lukewarm water. Rinse with a fresh sponge wrung out in clean lukewarm water. To dry, pat or daub the surface with a clean cloth. Change the washing solution and the rinse water as soon as either looks dirty.
- Always clean from the bottom of the wall upward. Wash only a small convenient-to-reach area at a time.

SCRUBBABLE WALL COVERINGS: What makes a wall covering "scrubbable" is a surface that has been coated with a protective finish, thus making the wall covering more stain resistant, durable, and capable of withstanding more vigorous washing.

Stain Removal

GREASE:
- If you can attend to a grease stain at once, you may be able to blot it up with an absorbent paper towel. Otherwise, make a paste by combining a nonflammable dry-cleaning solvent with an absorbent powder such as cornstarch or fuller's earth. Let the paste dry, then brush it off with a soft brush.
- Commercially made aerosol cleaners, made especially to clean wall coverings, may remove grease stains. Carefully follow the manufacturer's directions on the container. Usually, you can spray on the cleaner, let it dry, then brush it off along with the grease stain.

CRAYON MARKS:
- A sponge dipped in a commercial spot remover with dry-cleaning qualities will most often do the job.

INK: This is a difficult job when you're not certain of the type of ink involved.
- Always try to blot up the ink as fast as possible.
- Apply an absorbent powder such as cornstarch to the stain. As the powder absorbs the ink, brush it off and add more. It's important to work as quickly as possible.
- Commercially made ink eradicators are sold in many drug, stationery, and specialty stores. Be sure to test the eradicator on a small hidden area of the wall first, then follow the directions on the container.

8. WINDOWS AND WINDOW COVERINGS

At least once a week, as part of your regular housecleaning routine, use your vacuum's dusting attachment to draw dust from your window frames and sills, the curtains, and draperies. Also, dust the window shades, venetian blinds, or shutters.

Windows

Window Washing
Work goes faster if you have everything you need close by: a pail of clear warm water for washing, another pail with clear water for rinsing, washing cloths or sponges, soft cloths or chamois for drying, and a homemade cleaning solution or commercially made window-cleaning product.
- Put newspapers on the floor under all windows to catch any dust, dirt, or possible water splashes.

Crushed newspaper can be used to polish panes later on.
- Wipe very dirty panes with a dampened cloth to get rid of most of the soil before you begin to clean the windows.
- Commercially made aerosol sprays—generally quick, convenient and effective—are available. However, if you would like to make your own window cleaner, here are two well-tested, successful ways to make cleaning solutions, using common household products.

AMMONIA SOLUTION: Mix 2 tablespoons of *clear* household ammonia with 2 quarts of water. (This type of ammonia usually has the word "clear" written on the label, and underneath it is the statement "for windows and mirrors.") This is a good grease-cutting mixture. Don't let it drip on your woodwork, floors, or window hardware (especially on window hardware made of aluminum).

RUBBING-ALCOHOL SOLUTION: Mix 3–4 tablespoons of rubbing alcohol with 1 quart of warm water. During unusually cold or freezing weather, this solution will not form ice crystals. Dip a cloth or sponge in the cleaning solution and squeeze out just enough water to avoid dripping. Begin washing at the top of the window, so the cleaning solution won't drip onto previously cleaned areas.
- Wash one pane of glass at a time. Use a small brush, a cotton swab, or an old toothbrush to reach corner dirt. Wash large windows or a large expanse of glass by cleaning one area at a time. Use a clean cloth wrung out of clear water to rinse the washed area and a fresh clean cloth to dry the pane.

- When cleaning both sides of a window, use an up-and-down washing motion on the inside, and a side-to-side motion for the outside glass. This should enable you to see whether you missed cleaning any part of the glass and whether any streaks remain.
- Polish with a chamois or, if you prefer, a piece of crushed newspaper (which may take a bit longer but it does a good shiny job).
- To wash an outside window pane (from inside your house or apartment), use a squeegee-type product. Some have expandable rods that extend to about three feet. Look for the type that has a flat sponge on one end to do the washing and a firm, sharp-edged line of rubber on the other end to do the wiping. Place it against the window glass and pull it with one long stroke. Wipe the edge of the squeegee with a clean dry cloth after each downward pull. A long-handled self-wringing mop that's lightweight and easy to handle is another way to wash an outside window while remaining indoors.
- A razor-blade paint scraper can be used to carefully remove old paint stains from windows. (The paint-scraper holder holds a single-edged razor blade.) While some people soften old paint stains with turpentine, it usually isn't necessary when you use a paint scraper. Do not scratch the window glass with harsh abrasives such as steel-wool pads.
- Finish at each window by wiping the frame and the sill with a dampened cloth; then dry with a fresh one.
- To protect the sill from raindrops and other moisture hazards, you may wish to wax it. Use a wax suited to the type of paint on your sill, or a matching color for the wood. Follow directions on the container's label. In general, you can use a clean damp cloth to spread

on a thin even coating of wax, then let it dry thoroughly before hand rubbing it to a polished finish.

Window Coverings

Blinds

VENETIAN BLINDS: If you have any doubt as to how to clean your specific type of blind, first consult the retail dealer where you bought the blinds, or a venetian-blind maintenance firm. Some general cleaning instructions are:
- Dust venetian blinds regularly to keep them from becoming overly soiled. First, let them fall downward to their full length; then, with the dusting brush of the vacuum cleaner, start dusting at the top of the blinds, one side of the slats at a time. Then reverse the tilting mechanism and dust the other side of the slats. You can also use the dusting brush for the cords and tapes.

PAINTED OR PLASTIC BLINDS:
- To clean, use suds made of warm water and light-duty detergent as a cleaning solution. Wring a cloth out of the suds and wash both sides of each slat. To rinse, wring a cloth out of clear warm water and wipe the slat on both sides. Use a fresh cloth to dry.
- Change the wash water as soon as it becomes darkened; do the same with the rinse water.

NATURAL-WOOD BLINDS:
- Avoid using water on these blinds since it tends to warp or blister wood if left on for any period of time.
- Try using a creamy wax that's designed to clean and

wax at the same time. (Carefully read the container's label first.)
- If you wish, put on a pair of absorbent cleaning mitts when you apply the wax. By using both hands you may be able to clean and wax both sides of a slat at the same time.
- If you'd like the blinds to glisten, buff the slats with a soft cloth while the wax is still moist.

MATCHSTICK ROLL-UP BLINDS:
- Dust the blinds regularly with the dust-brush attachment of your vacuum cleaner or a soft cloth.
- For plastic matchstick blinds, a cloth wrung out of warm suds will wash away any soil. Follow with a cloth dampened in clear water to rinse thoroughly. Then dry with a fresh cloth.
- For bamboo roll-ups, wipe them with a damp cloth when necessary. Dry at once with a clean cloth. Do this on both sides of the blind.
- Do not submerge bamboo blinds in water as this could open up the "threads" and seriously damage the blind.
- Do not use soap or detergents to wash bamboo blinds. Also, never leave them in the sun. Both the detergents and the sun can damage the "binding threads."

Curtains

The amount of atmospheric pollutants in your locality, plus the amount of fumes in your home from a fireplace, furnace, or kitchen, are some of the determinants for how frequently washing or dry cleaning your curtains (and draperies) may be necessary. Because curtains are next to your window glass, they usually will need cleaning more often than draperies. Before cleaning, take off any removable hoops or metal clips. Read the manufacturer's instructions for safe handling.

Following are some general recommendations:
- To remove dust and particles of dirt, go over both sides of your curtains with a soft-bristled brush, or use the dusting tool of your vacuum cleaner. When dusting is done every week, they will not only look fresher but will wear longer.
- Soak very dirty sheer curtains for about 15 minutes in lukewarm water. Handle them carefully. Drain off the soak water and wash the curtains in a light-duty detergent in warm water. At all times use a squeezing motion, never a harsh twisting of the fabric. Rinse thoroughly.
- Machine-washable sheer and delicate curtain fabrics should be laundered in small loads. It's a safe idea to place them in a large mesh bag. Refer to the manufacturer's instructions for the right water temperature. Use the delicate washing cycle and wash gently for 2 to 3 minutes, or as directed in your washing-machine manual.
- Line dry sheer curtains, stretching the curtain as much as possible into its former shape. Or, dry briefly in the dryer and remove when slightly damp if light ironing is needed.
- Dry delicate lace or net curtains on a stretcher to bring them back into their original size and form.
- Hand wash most glass-fiber curtains (and draperies) in a good-sized tub. Use lukewarm water, add a mild detergent, and soak them for ½ hour, depending upon the amount of soil. Do not use chlorine bleach. Do not twist or wring because the fibers break easily

when wet. Be sure to wear protective gloves to move items around through the sudsy water to remove soil. Also, wear the gloves when you rinse out the tub in order to remove any possible fragments of glass from the tub's surface. Hang the curtains up to air dry.

Draperies

Follow the manufacturer's directions carefully for the recommended type of cleaning for your draperies. If you are uncertain whether the drapery material and its lining are washable, consult a reliable, professional dry cleaner. Also, have a reputable dry cleaner handle draperies made of fine fabrics such as damask, silk, velour, or velveteen.

For cleaning draperies at home, here are some general care suggestions:

- Dust each panel before cleaning. Use either a hand brush or the round dusting attachment of your vacuum cleaner. If this is done every week, your draperies will look fresher and wear longer.
- Lined draperies often require dry cleaning. However, if you know they are washable, colorfast, and preshrunk (referring to the lining, too), they can be hand-washed according to the type of fabric. Also, check the braid or trimming for washability, or remove it before washing the drapes.
- Do not overcrowd draperies in your washing machine. If they are too large, hand wash them in your bathtub.
- Refer to your washing machine's instruction manual for information on the right water temperature and washing cycle to use for draperies. In general, you should use a gentle washing cycle with about 6–8 minutes of wash time.

- Air dry draperies, if possible. Otherwise, use the dryer and remove the drapes while they are still slightly damp. Hang them up at once so that any wrinkles will smooth out.
- To hand launder glass-fiber draperies, see the previous section on "Curtains" in this chapter.

Screens

All screens need a routine dusting and cleaning when dirty. For the contemporary screen-and-storm-window combination, the dusting tool of your vacuum cleaner will suction up the dust and soil. To get specific information on their care, consult the professional installer at the time the windows are put in, or check in the Yellow Pages for a reputable firm. For cleaning:
- Dip a brush in warm detergent suds and go over the screen's mesh on both sides. Wash the frame in the same manner.
- To rinse, use a spray hose attached to a faucet, or pour warm clear water over the screen with a bucket. Turn the screen over and repeat rinsing it, to be certain that all the suds are removed. Have clean cloths handy so that you can dry the screens thoroughly.
- NOTE: Today's variety of materials used to make screening mesh includes bronze, copper, aluminum, steel, and plastic. Some are given an anti-rust treatment during manufacture. For screen mesh that is not rust-resistant, commercial products are available to help prevent rust and discoloration, or you can use spar varnish diluted with about 50 percent paint thinner. Use a paint brush to spread the thinned solution on both sides of your clean screens; give them time to dry thoroughly before using them or storing them away.

Shades

Consult a professional window cleaner for specific instructions on cleaning your particular type of shade. Dusting and occasionally wiping them with a damp cloth is a routine procedure to keep window shades clean.

An important feature to note is whether your window shade has been chemically treated at the factory to make it stain-resistant. In that case, your shade should need an overall cleaning only periodically.

- To clean most washable shades, remove one shade at a time from the wall, unroll it on a large flat surface, and wipe all surface dust with a soft cloth. Then use either a commercial foam cleaner (such as Big Wally) or wash with mild detergent suds and warm water.
- To clean non-washable shades, use a professional window-shade cleaning service, or possibly do it yourself. If the latter, unroll the shade on a large flat surface and clean it with a dough-type wall cleaner such as Absorene (available in paint, wall-coverings, or hardware stores) or with an art-gum eraser. To treat any soiled or stained areas, use the cleaner to brush the shade lightly from top to bottom with even strokes.

9. STAIN REMOVAL

You are apt to be more successful if you promptly treat a stain before it has dried and set. It's much more difficult, and sometimes impossible, to remove if you wait before taking action.

Before beginning to treat a stain, you should know what type of fabric you're dealing with. Refer to the manufacturer's care label for this information. Test all solutions first on sample swatches of material or an inconspicuous part of the article to make sure the fabric won't be harmed or the colors affected.

If you wish to use a professional dry cleaner, give him complete information about the type of stain, the fiber content of the fabric, how long ago the stain occurred, and stain-removal methods you've tried.

GENERAL PROCEDURES

Below are general recommendations for removing stains from upholstered furniture, carpets, draperies, and other fabrics:

- First blot up all excess wetness from the stain; scrape off as much solid matter as possible with a dull knife.
- Sponge gently with clear cold water. Rubbing is not advised; it only spreads the stain.

- Hold a clean white cloth or paper towel against the reverse side (if possible) of the fabric to absorb the stain while you work on the front with another clean white cloth or paper towel. Keep turning both the sponging and absorbing cloths so that only a clean surface touches the fabric, front and back.
- Work a stain from the edges inward toward the center, to prevent its spreading. Use light strokes.
- If you can work from the reverse side of the fabric (preferable for draperies, curtains, and slipcovers, but not rugs or carpets), hold several thicknesses of clean cloths or toweling against the face of the fabric and work the stain from the back, dabbing or sponging it out. Continue turning and changing the underneath cloth as well as the sponging cloth so that only clean surfaces touch the fabric, and the stain won't spread farther.
- Use an applicator or medicine dropper so that only a limited amount of the cleaning solution is dispensed; or wring a cloth out of the solution and apply to the stain. Never pour on a cleaning solution.

CLEANING SOLUTIONS

The following are some of the most commonly used solutions for stain removal. Use these solutions cautiously—testing a solution first before applying it to the stain.

Absorbent Powder (e.g., cornstarch, talcum, powdered whiting, powdered chalk, fuller's earth, cornmeal)
- Sprinkle absorbent powder on the stain. The absorbent can first be dampened with a dry-cleaning solvent to make a paste that is then tapped or gently rubbed into the stain and allowed to dry.

- Vacuum or gently brush up the residual powder.
- Test before using, especially on velvety fabrics or dark colors.

Ammonia Solution
- Add ¾ of a cup of tepid water to 1 tablespoon of ammonia.
- Use a plain, non-sudsy, non-detergent household ammonia without fragrance or added color.

Bleach
- For a chlorine bleach, add ½ cup of water to 1 tablespoon of bleach.
- Use a 3 percent solution of hydrogen peroxide.
- Never use bleach on carpets or upholstery.

Detergent Solution
- Add a few drops of a mild liquid detergent to ½ cup of lukewarm or cool water. This solution is commonly used for washing dishes and laundering delicate fabrics by hand. Apply only the suds; don't soak the fabric.
- For rugs, combine 1 teaspoon of detergent, 1 quart of warm water, and 1 teaspoon of white vinegar.

Dry-cleaning Solvent
- Before applying this solvent, make sure the fabric or rug is completely dry.
- Never pour a dry-cleaning solvent directly on fabric, so as not to overwet it. Use a special applicator or some toweling. Have a blotter under the spot on the fabric, if possible.

- Don't let the solvent come in contact with carpet or upholstery backing made of rubber latex or foam.

Vinegar Solution
- Add 1 cup of tepid water to ½ cup of white vinegar.

TYPES OF STAINS

Alcoholic Beverages
- Blot up any excess liquid. Sponge the stain promptly with cool water. Sponge with 1 part white vinegar to 3 parts cool water, then rinse. If the stain remains, rub detergent suds into it. Then rinse and blot dry.

Blood
- Blot up excess. Sponge gently with cool water in mild suds. Rinse with cool water. If the stain persists, sponge with a solution of 1 teaspoon of ammonia to 1 cup of cool water. Repeat the detergent treatment, then rinse. If the stain still remains, sponge with a 3 percent solution of hydrogen peroxide. (Test the solution first to make sure that the fabric can take this bleach.)
- Another suggestion is to gently rub a paste of cornstarch and cold water on the stained area. Allow it to dry; then brush it off lightly. Repeat the procedure, if necessary.

Candle Wax
- To chill the wax, rub it with an ice cube. Carefully scrape off the wax with a dull-edged knife. Place layers of facial tissue or paper towels over the spot. Press lightly with a warm iron to melt the wax. Blot up the melted wax. To remove any of the remaining

stain, sponge with a safe, nonflammable cleaning fluid.

Chewing Gum/Adhesive Tape
- Scrape off as much gum or tape as possible. Rub the stained area with ice. Remove any excess gummy matter carefully with a dull knife. Sponge the stain with a safe, nonflammable dry-cleaning fluid. Blot dry after each application.

Chocolate/Cocoa
- Sponge or scrape off excess solid matter. Sponge with tepid water, then with detergent suds (½ teaspoon detergent in 1 cup of tepid water). Rinse and blot thoroughly; then dry. If a greasy stain remains, sponge it with a safe, nonflammable dry-cleaning fluid.

Coffee/Tea
- Blot up the excess liquid. Sponge with tepid water. Apply detergent suds (1 cup of tepid water to 1 teaspoon of detergent) to the stain. Rinse and dry. If the grease stain remains, sponge with a safe, nonflammable dry-cleaning fluid.

Egg/Meat Gravy
- If the stain has dried on the fabric, scrape off as much as possible with a dull knife. Sponge with cool water. Then, sponge with tepid detergent suds. Dry thoroughly. You can also sponge the stain with a dry-cleaning solvent.

Fruits/Juices
- Sponge with cool water as soon as possible and blot dry. If the stain remains, sponge on mild detergent

suds. Rinse and dry thoroughly. If necessary, apply a chlorine bleach solution or sponge with a dry-cleaning solvent.

Grease/Oil (e.g., car grease, butter, mayonnaise, salad dressing)
- Scrape off excess with a dull knife. Sponge with a dry-cleaning solvent. Blot; don't rub the stain. Or, use a coarse absorbent like cornmeal.

Ink (ball-point)
- Try to remove the stain immediately. Sponge it with rubbing alcohol with the reverse side down over a pad of absorbent toweling. Dampen a folded piece of cloth in the alcohol and sponge lightly, working from the outside of the stain in. Blot immediately.
- Or, you can try a nonflammable stain remover. If the stain has dried or has set a long while, it may be quite difficult to remove.

Milk/Cream/Ice Cream
- Blot up any excess liquid and sponge with cool water. Then sponge in mild detergent suds and rinse thoroughly. If the grease stain remains, sponge with a safe, nonflammable cleaning fluid.

Mustard
- Scrape away any excess and sponge in mild detergent suds. Rinse. If the stain persists, use a safe, nonflammable dry cleaner. Repeat the treatment if the stain is still visible.

Rust
- Moisten the stain with cool water. Sponge in a lemon juice and table-salt solution. Rinse well. If the fabric

can take a bleach, try a sodium-perborate bleach (like Clorox 2). Since commercial rust removers contain toxic ingredients, it's best to get professional help.

Soft Drinks
- Sponge the stain immediately with cool water. Apply mild detergent solution suds and rinse. If necessary, when dry, dab with a pad saturated in a dry-cleaning solution.
- Some soft-drink stains when left to dry are invisible but turn yellow with aging. This type of yellow stain may be impossible to remove.

Urine/Pet Stains
- Sponge in the suds of a solution of 1 teaspoon of mild detergent, 1 teaspoon of white vinegar, and 1 quart of tepid water. Rinse the area well and dry. Repeat the procedure, if needed.

Vomit
- Scrape up any solids. Sponge with ¼ cup of table salt dissolved in 1 quart of tepid water. Rinse with clean water. Apply detergent suds and rinse. If necessary, apply an ammonia solution (1 teaspoon of non-sudsy, non-scented, non-colored ammonia in ¾ cup of tepid water). Rinse the area well and dry.

Wine
- Blot up excess liquid. Sponge with tepid water and club soda.
- Or, cover thickly with table salt or other absorbent for one hour. Then sponge on detergent solution suds. Rinse the area well and dry.

10. PEST CONTROL

Your primary defense to discourage unwelcome household pests is frequent and thorough cleaning of your home. When this does not provide sufficient protection, the good strong aim of the right pesticide for a specific pest is your best weapon.

PREVENTIVE MEASURES

Sealing Household Cracks
- Close up all possible entryways for any type of pest. Seal the cracks around metal pipes, water pipes, and drains in the kitchen and bathroom. Also, check for cracks around radiator and steam pipes and seal them.
- Before using a crack filler, scrub the area to be sealed up with hot suds. Wash away all traces of soap, grease, and dirt; then rinse completely and dry the surface thoroughly before using a crack filler.
- Several types of waterproof crack fillers are available. Read labels carefully to be certain the product will work successfully on a metal surface. One type is in powder form; you mix it at home using a small amount of powder at one time, with just enough water

to form a paste that can be applied with a spatula. Another type of crack filler is a plastic sealant that comes in a tube and is ready to apply in a slim ribbonlike stream along the crack.

- If you use a powdered crack filler, wash the container or bowl and spatula right after use, before the mixture becomes hard. Don't pour the excess down the drain; place it on old newspapers and dispose of it in the trash can. With the plastic sealant, wipe off immediately any excess that oozes outside the crack with a paper towel. (If you get any on your clothing, use a dry-cleaning fluid to remove it.) In both instances, follow the manufacturer's directions on the container's label.
- Fill in cracks in wood—between floorboards, around baseboards, in walls and moldings—with a repair material to which you add just enough water for it to have the consistency of putty. Use the amount you need to fill in the cracks with a slender spatula or an old knife. Make sure the container's label states that the putty will adhere to wood. When used outside the home, the putty must be kept painted on any exposed surface.
- Make sure that your windows and doors fit snugly. Also, see that the screens in your doors or windows are kept free of holes and tears.

Keeping Your Kitchen Clean
- Don't leave any food around your home. Clean up any liquid food spills, food crumbs on floors, tabletops, or children's trays at once.
- Keep kitchen drawers and food-storage cabinets well scrubbed since these areas are possible hideouts for pests. Clean behind any movable kitchen equipment and cabinets.

- Place garbage in plastic bags inside your kitchen garbage container and dispose of it frequently. Whether your garbage container is made of metal, rubber, or plastic, no matter how secure its lid is, if it is left in the home overnight, food odors will attract pests.
- Don't let dirty dishes stay in your sink or dishwasher overnight. Wash dishes as soon as possible after use.
- Foods should be protected in clean, tightly closed containers. When possible, keep your packaged dry foods stored on shelves in a somewhat cool area.
- Before buying prepackaged dry foods such as cereals, grains, flour, and dry-milk powder, check the packages carefully for evidence of openings in the package where insects could gain entry. Periodically check the outside and inside of dry-food packages you have stored for some time, and dispose of any that look as though they might be insect-infested. Also, check your spices. Paprika, chili powder, and red pepper tend to be somewhat oily, and should be kept in a cool place.
- Cartons such as those used by grocery stores to deliver food should not be kept in your home in case they should harbor insects or insect larvae.

General Household Cleaning Tips
- Empty wastebaskets daily as some types of pests, such as cockroaches, feed on paper.
- Keep closets clean.
- Scraps of fabric or pieces of lint in out-of-the-way corners may serve as nesting places for pests, another reason to keep your home immaculately clean.
- Don't leave food in your pet's dish overnight. Clean the area thoroughly where your pet eats or sleeps.

PESTICIDES

Although your home may be well-scrubbed and as clean as possible, there may be evidence of pests through no fault of your own. In that event, you will need the help of a good pesticide.

The term *pesticide* covers the various types of chemicals used to control pests. For example, an *insecticide* is a chemical used to control insects; a *miticide* is used to control mites; and a *rodenticide* is used to control rodents.

Pesticides are available in different forms for various purposes. *Surface sprays* are used to exterminate crawling insects; *aerosols* are air sprays to catch flying pests; and *dust sprays* can get into difficult-to-reach cracks and corners.

The two basic types—surface sprays and air sprays—differ in these ways: After a surface spray dampens or wets a surface, it dries, leaving a thin deposit of insecticide that remains for several weeks and will kill any insect that crawls over it. An air spray will kill a flying insect on contact; it is also used to drive insects out of hiding. Only flying insects hit directly with an air spray will be killed.

Usage of Pesticides

The following suggestions, courtesy of special booklets and handbooks published by the U. S. Department of Agriculture, are for your own and your family's safety when dealing with pesticides:

BEFORE USING PESTICIDES:
- *Read the label carefully before purchasing a pes-*

ticide. Registrations of pesticides are under constant review by the Environmental Protection Agency, so use only those pesticides that have the EPA registration number and that carry directions for home and garden use. Also, the label should plainly list the name of the kind of pest you are trying to eliminate.
- Check ingredients against the latest findings of the U. S. Department of Agriculture and the Environmental Protection Agency. Levels of safety are constantly changing.
- Follow the directions and the safety instructions on the pesticide container. Reread the label each time before using the pesticide. Do not depend upon your memory.
- Keep children, other adults, and pets away from areas where the pesticide will be used. Place poison baits (used for rats, ants, and roaches) out of the reach of children and pets.
- If the pesticide container is marked "Poison," read what the label recommends for you to do in case of an emergency. If some of the pesticide is swallowed, follow label directions and promptly call your doctor. If your doctor cannot be reached right away, it is important to get the poisoned victim to a hospital quickly. It's possible that one of your hospitals has a poison-control center. Keep these emergency telephone numbers handy near your telephone.

WHILE USING PESTICIDES:
- It is extremely important that none of the pesticide comes in contact with food, dishes, or cooking utensils in your home. Also, keep it away from your pet's food and water.
- Turn your face away from the container's cap when

you open it, and at all times keep the pesticide away from your face. Avoid breathing in pesticide sprays or dusts.
- Protect your hands by wearing plastic gloves.
- Don't smoke when using a pesticide. Even if its label says "nonflammable," don't take any chances. Do not eat, drink water or other beverages, or even chew gum, as some of the pesticide chemicals could get into your system.
- Keep the area where you are using a surface spray well ventilated and with the windows open. (During the winter, arrange for everyone, including pets, to leave the rooms for at least a half hour.)
- Never mix two different kinds of pesticides.
- Never try to siphon a pesticide from its container.
- If a pesticide's label states that it has an oil base, do not use the pesticide near a range with a gas pilot flame, an electric motor, or an electric circuit. The U. S. Department of Agriculture cautions that pesticides may soften and discolor some hard-surface floor coverings, such as vinyl, and other plastic materials in the home. Spray-test on an inconspicuous part of these areas before using the oil-based spray.
- A pesticide may cause damage to the underlying cement of a parquet floor. Apply lightly so that as little as possible seeps through any cracks in the floor.
- Before applying a space or aerosol spray, arrange for other adults, children, and pets to be out of the house for an hour or so. Any food outside the refrigerator, including your pet's food dishes, should be kept far away from where any spraying will take place. Close all windows and doors before spraying a pesticide so that the fumes will not spread through the house.

Leave your home after spraying the infested areas; thoroughly air dry the rooms upon your return.

AFTER USING PESTICIDES:
- After using a pesticide, be sure to give your face and hands a thorough wash with soap and water. Don't allow pesticides to remain on your skin or clothing. If spills do occur, remove your clothes at once and have them laundered before wearing them again.
- Dispose of the pesticide container when you have finished using its contents. Wrap it completely in newspapers, tie the bundle tightly, and put it in a trash can with its lid securely on. Never dispose of it in an incinerator, and never put a pesticide near intense heat.
- To store pesticides, keep the containers tightly closed. If just a small amount of the pesticide is left, don't be tempted to put it in a smaller container. Keep a pesticide in its original container, with its label intact.
- Do not keep a pesticide container if its label has been lost. Dispose of it immediately. Pesticide containers should not be kept under the kitchen sink, in bathroom medicine cabinets, food-storage cabinets, or anywhere near food. Because the products are hazardous to children and pets, put pesticides in a cabinet with a good sturdy lock on it (if possible), out of their reach.

TYPES OF HOUSEHOLD PESTS

In addition to the suggestions made on pest control in the following paragraphs, you may need more specific information for your pest-control problems. If so, consult a professional pest-control operator in your area.

Ants

An ant is distinguishable from a termite by its outline: an ant has an hourglass shape (pinched in at the waist), and a termite's body is pole straight. There are various types and sizes of ants: red, brown, black, ranging in size from one-sixteenth of an inch to one-tenth of an inch. (The carpenter ant, however, may be as long as a half inch.)

Ants love food, especially sugar and sugary foods such as cake and cookie crumbs. Usually they will not attack clothing or other textiles or leather items. Some types of ants, such as the carpenter ant, will bore into the rotting woodwork of an old home, looking for moisture. They may not eat the wood they are damaging, but will grind it into minute particles, then carry these tiny bits of wood away to build their nests. This type of damage could eventually weaken certain parts of a building's structure.

- Watch to see the direction in which ants carry their food, when attempting to locate their nest.
- If the ants' nest is indoors, spray it with a liquid household insecticide. If the nest is outdoors, put caulking compound on cracks and other openings where ants might possibly enter the house. Be sure to spray the lower part of window frames, around doors, the cracks in baseboards, floors, walls, and cracks around bathtubs and toilets. Be careful that there are no household pets in the area of the spray. Ant traps, available in hardware stores, can also be effective.
- Clean areas in back of kitchen appliances. Also, clean any movable cupboards and storage cabinets so you can get in behind. Then apply an insecticide. It may be easier to treat specific sites if you use a cream or paste insecticide and a paintbrush to do the job.

Bats

This mouselike flying mammal has a furry body, usually brown in color, and membranous wings that it flaps as it flies at night. Bats will fly into your home through any entrance left open to them in order to find an unused quiet space (such as your attic or an upper storage room) where they can roost during the day.

Bats are subject to rabies, an often-fatal disease that may be transmitted to people. Bats can make eerie screeching sounds as they fly and have an objectionable odor.

Since it may be necessary to fumigate the infested area, this job should be done by a professional exterminator. Afterward, the area should be aired out and cleaned thoroughly.

- Any openings to lofts where bats may enter should be covered with sheet metal, or ¼-inch-mesh hardware cloth.
- Never handle a live bat; you could be exposed to rabies. If you have to pick up a dead bat to dispose of it, be sure to wear rubber gloves.

Bedbugs

Bedbugs are brown, flattish insects between ¼ and ⅜ inch long. They are usually visible only as black or brown spots on bed linen, walls, or other areas near the bed. Bedbugs produce an unpleasant odor, and their bite causes itching. Usually they move about at night.

- Thoroughly spray bed slats, springs, and frames with an insecticide containing lindane, malathion, ronnel, or pyrethrum. Applications of pyrethrum may be necessary several times during one- to two-week inter-

vals. If you use lindane, ronnel, or malathion, usually only one spraying is necessary.
- NOTE: The U. S. Department of Agriculture suggests caution with sprays containing lindane or malathion. Always check the container's label before using.
- Once bedbugs are in a mattress, it's best to purchase a new mattress, rather than spraying into the seams and tufts of the mattress itself.

Book Lice

These tiny, transparent insects like homes with a lot of humidity. They move about at night and feed upon the sizing (binding substance) of paper stored at high humidities and warm temperatures, starched clothing, or linens.
- Ventilate the infested areas, remove dust, and spray with a malathion solution or dust.

Carpet Beetles

Among the four different species of carpet beetles, the adult black carpet beetle is the only type with a solid black body and brownish legs. Its larvae are yellowish, golden, or dark brown. Its body, about ½ inch long, is tapered from beginning to end, where there is a tuft of long brown hair.

The three other species of carpet beetles, when adult, have mottled colorings of white, brown, yellow, or black. Their larvae, elongate and oval, have brownish or black bristles, and are a bit shorter than the black beetles. They grow to be ¼ inch in length.

Among the items the larvae of carpet beetles (and clothes moths) feed on are carpets, rugs, draperies, upholstery, feather or down pillows, hair mattresses, and

woolen blankets. They will also feed on clothing made of fur, wool, or mohair, and brush bristles and hair.
- To control carpet beetles, vacuum carpets and rugs regularly. (Today most woolen carpets and rugs have been treated with an insect-proofing process in the factory. If your woolen floor coverings need this protective treatment, call a reliable professional carpet-and-rug-cleaning service for help.)
- Rotate rugs periodically to rout out insects under heavy pieces of furniture.
- Use the dusting tool of your vacuum cleaner to clean draperies and upholstered furniture. Empty the vacuum bag as soon as possible in case it has drawn in any insects, eggs, or larvae.
- To protect your household furnishings and clothing from the carpet beetle (and the clothes moth), spray with a non-staining household insecticide. Read the label and follow directions carefully. The pesticide should contain methoxychlor or perthane.

Centipedes

These long-legged wormlike pests feed on other small insects but should not harm your food or furnishings.
- Spray centipedes and their hiding places with a surface spray of lindane.

Clothes Moths

The two different species of clothes moths, when fully adult, are quite similar; they are yellowish or buff in color, and have a wingspread of about ½ inch. The fully grown larvae are white and have dark heads. (They look like worms, and have no wings.) In length, they are about ½ inch.

- To control clothes moths, clean your closets regularly. Keep them well aired, well dusted, and all items clean and well brushed.
- Do not assume that a natural fiber, such as wool, when combined with a synthetic fiber, is protected from danger. Moths (or carpet beetles) will instinctively pick out the wool threads to feed on, and may make a lacelike sieve out of your fabric.
- One way to protect your woolens is to wash or dry clean soiled items, then spray them with a non-staining insecticide. While dry cleaning will kill moths (and carpet beetles), it is not a guarantee against future damages. If you plan to store a woolen item, spray it again with the insecticide before putting it away. To do this, hang each piece of clothing separately over a shower rod—or outdoors on a clothesline, if possible. Spray lightly and uniformly with a non-staining insecticide. Use just enough spray to get the surface moist; do not soak or saturate the item. Too much spray will leave a white deposit when the fabric dries. You can brush off the slight excess spray.
- Another method to protect woolens during the summer is to store them in a closet in which you place mothballs or crystals.
- Unseen places where moths may be hiding are behind radiators, in corners, cracks, baseboards, and moldings. These places should be cleaned, then treated with a surface spray containing malathion or ronnel, lindane or diazinon.

Cockroaches, Waterbugs

Cockroaches are adept at hiding during the day, then emerging at night to locate food and water, contaminating what they find. In addition, cockroaches will eat anything containing starch or glue, including starched fabrics, books, or papers.

The five species of cockroaches found in homes in the United States range from ½ to 2 inches in length, and from yellowish or reddish-brown to black.

Cleanliness in your home is very important to discourage the existence and spread of cockroaches. If roaches do become a problem, however, a good insecticide is your best protection. Chlorpyrifos, diazinon, malathion, propoxur, or ronnel insecticides will control all kinds of cockroaches. Lindane will also control these pests, except possibly the German cockroach, which has developed a resistance to lindane in some parts of the country.

- Use a household surface spray and a dust in cracks and openings around your home where roaches may hide. Use a household spray gun, or a surface spray sold in pressurized cans. Moisten the surface thoroughly, but not so much that the liquid will drip or run. To force roaches out into the open, use a space spray or aerosol mist containing pyrethrin to get down deep into cracks and crevices. Usually this won't kill the pest but will drive it out where you can eliminate it with a surface spray or dust.
- Another method is to place roach traps in areas where roaches have been sighted. Children and pets should not be allowed near the traps.
- Before applying the insecticide, remove all food, dishes, and shelf paper from your cupboards. See that your shelves are empty and clean. Then remove any drawers and all utensils to avoid contamination by the spray or powder. (It's very important to give the spray time to dry thoroughly before you relay clean

shelf paper and replace any food items. Use nonporous shelf paper as an additional precaution.)
- Other places to apply the insecticide are:
  (1) underneath cupboards and cabinets; in all possible cracks and crevices. (Remove all contents first.)
  (2) on the sides, backs, and bottoms of drawers. Keep drawers scrupulously clean, and do not put insecticide on the inside of drawers.
  (3) under the kitchen sink and the drainboard, and along exterior wall pipes.
  (4) behind the refrigerator/freezer, range, dishwasher.
  (5) on the undersides of tables and chairs.
  (6) behind loose baseboards, molding strips, window or door frames.
  (7) on the interior of a closet that has been emptied and cleaned.
  (8) on bookshelves, where books have been removed and the shelves have been cleaned.
  (9) behind electric wall clocks.

Crickets

In the country or rural areas, the field cricket can become a nuisance in the home during late summer after the crops have been harvested. At that time it seeks the warmth and food available indoors. The house cricket is even in evidence in cities where they may breed in outdoor refuse heaps before entering houses during the summer months. Crickets can damage clothing and other fabrics.
- To protect your home, seal any openings leading into the house where crickets could gain entry. Screens, windows, and doors should fit snugly.

- Apply a spray insecticide around baseboards, in cracks where a cricket might hide, and in closets.
- Use a dust spray for the bare concrete floor of a basement room.

Fleas

These pests are a nuisance to people as well as animals, mostly dogs. By sucking blood, they cause an itchy, painful bite that may last for several days or a week.

Fleas are easily spread around a home. First, the female flea lays eggs on your pet. The eggs hatch wherever the pet goes: to its own bed, one of your finest chairs, the sofa, rug, or carpet. Larval fleas that hatch from eggs may grow to maturity in unseen crevices in the floor.

- Keep all rooms clean. Vacuum carpets, rugs, upholstered furniture, and other places where eggs or larvae may be.
- Apply a household insecticide surface spray containing methoxychlor, malathion, pyrethrin, or ronnel. Use a non-staining insecticide for spraying carpets, rugs, and upholstered furniture. Check the label carefully.
- Spray any cracks in the floor, the lower parts of walls, baseboards, and the area where your pet sleeps. If necessary, spray again around your home after about a week.
- One method to control fleas on your pets is to use an insecticide dust containing malathion, or methoxychlor. This should be safe and effective when applied directly into the dog's or cat's fur, right to the skin. Follow the directions on the insecticide label.
- It's best not to put a flea collar on your pet for the

first time without consulting a veterinarian. Its skin may be too tender to withstand the collar. Before using any flea powders, soaps, or shampoos on your pet, take it to a veterinarian to test for possible allergies and to find out which flea remedies are best for your particular pet.

Flies

In addition to being a nuisance, flies also pose a health hazard by feeding on garbage or on food carelessly left on your table, then contaminating everything they touch and spreading many human diseases. Therefore, it is very important to keep clean and see that no garbage is allowed to accumulate in the areas where flies might breed.

- Keep garbage cans covered with snug-fitting lids. Outdoor garbage cans should be emptied at least once a week, more often during the summer. Kitchen garbage should not be left in the house overnight. Dispose of pet droppings promptly.
- Cover all food. Don't leave food where it will attract flies.
- Use screens in windows and doors. A screen with 14 meshes to the inch will keep out flies; a screen with 16 meshes to the inch should keep out smaller insects.
- Apply a household aerosol spray made specifically for flying insects if you need more than a fly swatter. Follow label directions carefully.

Gnats

The gnat is a tiny two-winged insect that is part of the mosquito species. Some gnats bite or sting.
- Use an aerosol spray specifically for flying insects.

- Remove water from vases or from rain gutters before it becomes stagnant.

Mice

Holes in walls, floors, and in house foundations should be sealed off to keep mice outside your home. In addition to contaminating food, mice can gnaw into fabrics and wood, as well as transmit human diseases.

- One suggestion is to put mouse traps along walls and near holes where mice could enter your home. You may wish to bait traps with foods with tempting odors, such as peanut butter, bacon, or cheese. Don't permit young children or your pets to go near the traps. One type of trap you can purchase, called Havahart, catches the mouse unharmed.
- When there are so many mice that trying to trap them is not practical, some homeowners resort to poison baits. These materials can be dangerous to humans, so if used, all the directions and precautions on the container's label must be followed *exactly as stated*. Poison baits must be placed where they won't contaminate foods, or cause serious harm. Generally this method is used for outside purposes.
- The safest way to control an infestation of mice is to call a qualified pest-control service. A professional exterminator should have the right equipment to solve your type of problem.

Mites

Mites are tiny, almost microscopic insects but they can cause itching and swollen flesh (welts) in people. Some species, such as clover mites, won't bite; others, such as rodent or bird mites, will. The latter are drawn to homes where rats, mice, or pet birds are present.

According to the U. S. Department of Agriculture, food mites (sometimes called *weevils*) breed in certain foods such as cheese and grains, and can cause skin rash when they get on people.

- A repellent, containing deet, ethyl hexanediol, or dimethyl phthalate, can be used to control mites outdoors. These miticide sprays are usually available in hardware or sporting-goods stores. Read the label on the container carefully before using.
- For general use around the home, a household surface spray containing malathion can be used to control mites.
- If your food cupboard shelves are still infested with mites after a thorough cleaning (washing with hot water and detergent, then rinsing), use a household surface spray containing not more than 2 percent malathion. Take special care not to contaminate food or cooking utensils with the insecticide. Let the spray dry thoroughly, then cover your shelves with clean moisture-proof paper.

Mosquitoes

The tiny two-winged mosquito is known for its aggressive buzz, its biting sting, and its capacity to suck blood from people and animals. The female lays her eggs in stagnant water, such as puddles, gutters, rain barrels, pools, or saucers under a potted plant.

Some mosquitoes are disease carriers, and since stagnant water is necessary for their breeding, one way to control them is to eliminate their breeding places and see that all water containers are kept filled with fresh water.

Usually mosquitoes are attracted to light sources

(lamps, TV screens), making it easy to note their presence.
- To kill mosquitoes inside your home, use an aerosol spray specifically for flying insects. Follow the manufacturer's directions on the container's label carefully.
- Keep fresh water in flower vases. See that the water from potted plants that drips into a saucer is removed and does not become stagnant.
- Outdoors, see that rain gutters are freed of old leaves and soil. Don't allow pools to collect debris. If you have a rain barrel, see that its cover is secure when it's not catching rain water.

Moths
- See "Clothes Moths" in this chapter. Moths can also harm carpets, rugs, draperies, lamp shades, as well as clothes in your home.

Rats
- Seal up holes in all outside walls; do not leave food uncovered, and dispose of all garbage promptly.
- Many of the general precautions given for controlling mice also apply to controlling rats. However, since a rat can be vicious, it's wise not to try to handle the problem all by yourself. Seek professional help from an exterminator and/or your local board of health.

Roaches (See Cockroaches.)

Scorpions
In appearance, the scorpion looks somewhat like a very small lobster, has four legs, and a front pair of nipping claws, with a long, slender, jointed tail ending

in a curved poisonous stinger. Scorpions usually are found in the southern portions of the United States. They grow to be 10 inches in length. They like sandy areas; also moisture. They usually hide where there's water at night, and during the day may turn up in an attic, closet, or even in blankets, shoes, or a stack of newspapers.
- Do not let your children play in sandy areas, such as beach fronts, that are not well tended. If you or a family member is stung by a scorpion, call your doctor at once.
- To control scorpions, use a household surface spray containing lindane. Spray around windows, door casings, along baseboards, and around the foundation of the house. Also, spray the lower part of tree trunks, stumps, lumber, and rock walls. (Government researchers on pest control suggest that a water-based spray is preferable for outdoor use since ready-to-use household sprays often contain oils that might burn plant life and other types of vegetation.)

Silverfish/Firebrats

These two insects are similar in appearance: neither has wings; each is about ⅓ to ½ inch long. The silverfish is rather shiny, in a silver or pearl-gray tone; the firebrat is mottled gray.

Both insects hide out during the day and emerge at night to damage your food and clothes. Silverfish prefer cool, damp places, such as basements; firebrats like warm areas, such as the attic in summer and the furnace area in winter.
- All openings in walls or floors should be sealed to impede the movement of these insects around the house.
- Both insects will contaminate foods and are espe-

cially drawn to foods that are high in protein, sugar, or starch, especially cereals and moist wheat flour. Anything on which there is glue or paste, such as wall coverings and book bindings, attracts silverfish and firebrats. Also, if there is starch in any of your clothing, rayon fabrics, or table linens, these will attract the insects.

- For an insecticide, use either a surface spray containing lindane, diazinon, ronnel, malathion, or propoxur; or use a dust spray. First, read the label on the container carefully. If you apply the insecticide correctly, it will leave a residue that becomes ineffective after a few weeks. Repeat the procedure if it hasn't done the job effectively within two or three weeks.
- Spray around all the areas where you sight the insects, especially around pipes, on baseboards, door and window casings, and closets.
- If it's necessary only to eliminate insects from the warmer areas of your home, do not use a spray with an oil-based solution (check the label carefully), as oil-based solutions should not be applied near gas pilot flames or electric motors. Use a dust spray instead, containing not more than 1 percent lindane or 5 percent malathion.
- Apply the dust with a hand duster into cracks and on the surfaces of places recommended for sprays. (The U. S. Department of Agriculture states that dusts may be applied safely to areas where oil-solution sprays might start fires.)

Spiders

The black widow spider is ½ inch long; with a globe-shaped body; long, slender legs; and a poisonous bite. Call a doctor immediately if someone is bitten.

The black widow usually lurks in areas such as a seldom-used basement, beneath lawn benches, under the porch, a pile of old trash, in the garage, tool shed, or sand box.

The brown recluse spider is small, only about 3/8 of an inch long, but treacherous. Its bite can cause sores that are slow to heal. Call your doctor at once if someone is bitten.

To control spiders in and around the home, here are some suggestions:

- Clean up your yard. Remove any loose bricks, old lumber, broken outdoor furniture, or trash. Clean out any clutter in your basement where spiders may hide.
- Use a stick or broom with a cloth firmly covering its base to brush away spider webs, their egg sacs, and the spiders themselves from ceiling and corner areas.
- Apply a household spray containing lindane to all areas where spiders have been sighted, plus the areas mentioned above.
- Don't shoot the spray directly over your head since a spider hit by the spray could drop down on you. (Also, cover your hair.) Stand back a bit when you spray.
- If you see several spiders in their nests, have someone help with the eliminating procedure. If the number of nests seems overwhelming, get a professional exterminator.

Termites

There are two major kinds of termites: subterranean and non-subterranean. Both cause wood destruction. Subterranean termites live in nests in the ground and tunnel upward to reach the wood structure above. Non-subterranean termites live above the ground and can fly. They damage furniture, posts, piles of lumber, and structural timber.

Colonies of termites live in cavities they have made in wood, which could be a piece of your finest furniture. They work inside wood, and you may not know what is happening until you see the result of a termite's destruction of your property.

- To exterminate these destructive pests, call an experienced, reputable pest-control operator who has the necessary equipment to do the job. Dealing with termites is *not* a do-it-yourself project.

Ticks

Usually your dog unknowingly brings the brown dog tick into your home. After feeding on the dog (sucking its blood), the ticks hide under carpets, rugs, upholstered furniture, behind baseboards, and in cracks.

- Have a reliable veterinarian treat the dog to relieve its discomfort. Get the veterinarian's advice on what you can do to make your dog more comfortable by means of special powders or sprays it can be treated with the next time it is attacked by ticks.
- Use a household insecticide containing lindane, malathion, or diazinon to spray the area where your dog sleeps. Have your pet sleep elsewhere until the spray dries. It's a good idea also to spray areas where ticks might hide, such as in window casings and around cracked floorboards and baseboards. After two or three treatments, repeat the spraying procedure, if necessary.
- To destroy ticks hiding in or under carpets, rugs, and upholstered furniture, use a malathion spray that's guaranteed to be non-staining. (Check the container's

label so that the spray you use doesn't harm your furnishings.)

Wasps and Hornets

The wasp, with its slim body attached to an abdomen by a narrow "stalk," has a sharp biting mouth. The females have a vicious sting. Depending on the species, wasps can be black, reddish-brown, blue-black, or yellow, usually with cross-wise bands. Hornets are also stinging insects, and are yellow and black.

These flying insects may nest in an unoccupied building, under the eaves, under a porch ceiling, in shrubs, or on the lawn around a house. To kill them in their nests, any treatment should be done when there is not much activity around the nests and you are less likely to be stung.

- If only a few wasps or hornets are flying around, a special pesticide for these insects should be used. Only use a pesticide that has directions for use in or around the home.
- When the nests of wasps and hornets are sighted, call a special exterminator to handle the situation. He will come equipped with protective clothing and headgear to spray the area.
- If any member of your family has an allergy, asthma, or hayfever, and is stung by a wasp or hornet, call your doctor immediately.

INDEX

Absorbent powder for stain removal, 113–14
Accessories, 70–78
Acrylic plastic accessories, 75–76
Adhesive tape stains, 116
Aerosol sprays, 122
Aids for cleaning, 8–15
  safety suggestions, 15–17
Air-conditioners, 35–37
Air-conditioning systems, central, 36–37
Air filters, 35–37
Air sprays, 122
Alcohol, rubbing, for window washing, 104–5
Alcoholic beverage stains, 115
Aluminum
  bleaches and, 6
  cookware, 47
American Institute for Conservation of Historic and Artistic Works, The (AIC), 78
Ammonia, 3–5
Ammonia solution
  for stain removal, 114
  for window washing, 104
Ants, 126

Appliances, kitchen
  major, 18–27
  small, 27–35
Artwork, 78–80

Baking soda, 2
Ball-point stains, 117
Bamboo furniture, 65
Baseboards, 99
Basins, wash, 38–39
Bathmats, 41
Bathroom fixtures and furnishings, 38–41
Bathtubs, 38–39
Bats, 127
Bedbugs, 127–28
Beetles, carpet, 128–29
Black widow spiders, 139–40
Bleaches, 5–6
  for stain removal, 6, 114
Blenders, 28
Blinds, window, 106–7
Blood stains, 115
Bone china, 56–57
Book lice, 128
Books, 81–82
Braided rugs, 96
Brass accessories, 70–72
Brick floors, 83

143

Broilers
  electric, 23
    toaster-broilers, 34–35
  gas, 25
Bronze sculpture, 79–80
Brooms, 8–9
Brushes, 10–11
  vacuum cleaner, 14–15
Building Stone Institute, 86
Bulbs (incandescent), 41

Candle wax stains, 115–16
Cane furniture, 65
Can openers, electric, 28–29
"Care of Books, Documents, Prints and Films," 73, 81–82
Carpet beetles, 128–29
Carpets, 83, 92–95
  mildew on, 94
  removing stains from, 112–13
  types of, 95
  underpadding of, 94
Carpet sweepers, 12–13
Cast-iron cookware, 47–48
Ceilings, 98–102
  major cleanup, plan of action for, 98
  painted, 99
  stain removal, 101–2
Centipedes, 129
Central air-conditioning systems, 36–37
Ceramic-glass cookware, 50–51
Ceramic-glass ranges, 25–26
Ceramic tile floors, 86–87
Chamois cloths, 12
Chandeliers, crystal, 43–44
Chewing gum stains, 116

Chinaware, 56–57
Chlorine bleach, 5–6
Chocolate stains, 116
Chrome
  accessories, 72
  furniture, 67
Chromium-plated fittings, 39
Cleaners, commercial, 6–8
Cleaning solutions for removing stains, 113–15
Clothes moths, 129–30
Cloths, 11–12
  chamois, 12
Cockroaches, 130–32
Cocoa stains, 116
Coffee pots, electric, 29–30
Coffee stains, 116
Collectibles, 70–82
  accessories, 70–78
  artwork, 78–80
  books, 81–82
  fabric and fabric crafts, 80–81
  removing stains from, 112–13
Continuous-cleaning ovens, 26
Cookware, 45–53
  non-stick finishes, 46
  seasoning, 47–48
  types of, 46–53
Cooling equipment, 35–37
Copper
  accessories, 70–72
  cookware, 49
Cords, electrical, care of, 16–17
Cork floors, 84, 91
Cotton carpeting, 95
Countertops, 38–39
Cracks, sealing, 119–20

Crayon marks, removal of, 101
Cream stains, 117
Crevice tools, 14
Crickets, 132–33
Crystal
  accessories, 72–73
  chandeliers, 43–44
Curtains, 107–9
  shower, 41
Cutlery, 53–54

Decorative objects, 70–82
  accessories, 70–78
  artwork, 78–80
  books, 81–82
  fabric and fabric crafts, 80–81
    removing stains from, 112–13
Decorative pillows, 81
Defrosting refrigerators, 19–20
Dehumidifiers, 37
Detergents, 6–7
Detergent solutions for stain removal, 114
Diffusers, light, 42
Dinnerware, 56–57
Dishwasher detergents, 7
Dishwashers, 18–19
Dishwashing, hand, 54–55, 56
Door frames, 99
Draperies, 107–10
  removing stains from, 112–13
Dry-cleaning solvent for stain removal, 114–15
Dry method of cleaning carpets, 93
Dusting brushes, 14

Dusting cloths, 11–12
Dustpans, 9
Dust sprays, 122

Earthenware, 56–57
  accessories, 76
Egg stains, 116
Electrical cords, care of, 16–17
Electric appliances. *See* Appliances, kitchen; names of appliances
Electric ranges, 22–23
Emergency telephone numbers, 15, 123
Enamelware, 49–50
Environmental Protection Agency (EPA), 123
Equipment
  cooling, 35–37
  heating, 35–36
  home safety, 37–38
  humidifying, 37

Fabric crafts, 80–81
Fabrics, 80–81
  removing stains from, 112–13
Fans, electric, 37
Faucets, bathroom, 39
Fiber crafts, 80–81
Filters, air, 35–37
Finishes
  cookware, non-stick, 46
  furniture, special, 67–69
Firebrats, 138–39
Fire extinguishers, 15
Fittings, chromium-plated, 39
Fixtures, lighting, 41–44
Flammable liquids, 16

Flatware
  gold-plated, 57–58
  pewter, 58
  silver, 58–59
  stainless steel, 59–60
Fleas, 133–34
Flies, 134
Floor brushes, 14
Floor coverings. *See* Carpets; Rugs
Floors, 83–92
  bathroom, 40–41
  See also types of floors
Floor-waxing machines, 91
Fluorescent tubes, 42
Foam spray method of cleaning carpets, 93–94
Food processors, 30
Framed fabrics, 80–81
Frames
  door, 99
  mirror, 74
  window, 99
Freezers, 19–21
Fruit stains, 116–17
Frypans, electric, 30–31
Furniture, 61–69
  finishes and surfaces, special, 67–69
  polishing, 61–62
  removing stains from, 112–13
  types of, 61–67
Furniture nozzles, 14

Gas broilers, 25
Gas ranges, 23–25
Gilt accessories, 73
Glass
  accessories, 72–73
  ceramic cookware, 50–51
  ceramic ranges, 25–26
  cookware, 50–51
  covered pictures, 79
  furniture, 67
Glassware, 57
Gloves, waterproof household, 7–8
Gnats, 134–35
Gold accessories, 73
Gold-plated flatware, 57–58
Graphic art prints, 78–79
Gravy stains, 116
Grease stains, 101, 117

Hanging fixtures, light, 44
Heating equipment, 35–36
Home safety equipment, 37–38
Hooked rugs, 96
Hornets, 142
Humidifying equipment, 37

Ice cream stains, 117
Incandescent bulbs, 41
Ink eradicators, 102
Ink stains, 102
  ball-point, 117
Insecticides, 122

Juice stains, 116–17

Kitchen appliances
  major, 18–27
  small, 27–35
Kitchen knives, 53–54
Kitchens, keeping clean for pest control, 120–21
Knife blades, 53–54
Knives
  electric slicing, 33
  kitchen, 53–54

Labeling cleaning products,
    15–16
Lacquered objects,
    accessories, 71
    silver, 77
Lamps, 42
Lamp shades, 42–43
Leather
    accessories, 73
    upholstery, 64
Lice, book, 128
Light diffusers, 42
Lighting fixtures, 41–44
Light shields, 42
Liquids, flammable, 16
Lucite
    accessories, 75–76
    furniture, 68–69

Marble
    accessories, 74
    floors, 84–86
    furniture, 67–68
    sculpture, 79
    white vinegar and, 3
Matchstick roll-up blinds, 107
Meat gravy stains, 116
Mice, 135
Microwave ovens, 25–27
Mildew, 94
Milk stains, 117
Mirrors, 74
    bathroom, 39–40
Mites, 135–36
Miticides, 122
Mixers, electric, 31–32
Mops, 9–10
Mosquitoes, 136–37
Moths, 137
    clothes, 129–30
Mustard stains, 117

Natural-wood blinds, 106–7
Needlepoint panels, 80
Non-stick finishes on
    cookware, 46

Oil stains, 117
Organs, 66
Oriental rugs, 96–97
Outdoor carpeting, 95
Ovens
    cleaning systems, 26–27
    electric ranges, 22–23
    gas ranges, 23–24
    microwave, 25–27
Oxygen bleach, 5

Pads, wax-applicator, 12
Pails, 10
Painted blinds, 106
Painted ceilings, 99
Painted walls, 99
Painted wood furniture, 63
Paintings, 78–79
Paneling, wall, 99–100
Papered walls, 100–1
Pest control, 119–42
    pesticides, 122–25
    preventive measures,
        119–21
        general cleaning tips, 121
        keeping kitchen clean,
            120–21
        sealing cracks, 119–20
        types of pests, 125–42
Pesticides, 122–25
Pests, types of, 125–42
Pewter
    accessories, 75
    flatware, 58
Photographs, 78–79
Pianos, 66

147

Pictures, 78–79
　glass-covered, 79
Pillows, decorative, 81
Plastic laminate furniture, 68
Plastics
　blinds, 106
　furniture, 68
　rigid acrylic, accessories, 75–78
　washable, 43
Plasticware, 56–57
Plexiglass
　accessories, 75–76
　furniture, 68–69
Polishes, 8, 61–62
Porcelain
　accessories, 76
　chinaware, 56–57
Porcelain-coated cast-iron cookware, 48
Pottery, 76
Powdered cleaners, 8
Pressure cookers, 32–33
Prints, graphic art, 78–79
Products for cleaning, 1–8
　labeling, 15–16
　safety suggestions, 15–17

Quarry tile floors, 87

Range hoods, 26–27
Ranges, 21–25
　electric, 22–23
　gas, 23–25
　glass-ceramic, 25–26
Rats, 137
Rattan furniture, 65
Reed furniture, 65
Refrigerators, 19–21
　defrosting, 19–20

Roaches, 130–32
Rodenticides, 122
Rubbing alcohol for window washing, 104–5
Rugs, 92, 95–97
　mildew on, 94
　small, 80
　types of, 95–97
Rust stains, 39, 117–18

Safety
　cleaning products and aids, 15–17
　equipment, 37–38
Sal (washing) soda, 5
Scorpions, 137–38
Screens, window, 110
Sculpture, 79–80
Sealing cracks, 119–20
Seasoning cookware, 47–48
Self-cleaning ovens, 26
Shades
　lamp, 42–43
　window, 111
Shag rugs, 97
Shields, light, 42
Shower curtains, 41
Shower heads, 39
Silver
　accessories, 77
　bleaches and, 6
　and wood, 77
Silverfish, 138–39
Silverware, 58–59
Skillets, electric, 33–34
Slate floors, 86
Slicing knives, electric, 33
Smoke detectors, 37–38
Soda
　baking, 2
　washing (sal), 5

Soft drink stains, 118
Solvent, dry-cleaning, for stain removal, 114–15
Solvent-soaked cloths, 11–12
Spiders, 139–40
Sponge mops, 10
Sponges, 10
Sprays, pesticide, 122
Stainless steel
  cookware, 51–52
  knife blades, 53–54
  tableware, 59–60
Stain removal, 101–2, 112–18
  cleaning solutions for, 113–15
  general procedures for, 112–13
Stains, types of, 115–18
Stereos, 66
Stoneware, 56–57
String mops, 9–10
Surfaces, special, 67–69
Surface sprays, 122
Sweepers, carpet, 12–13

Tableware, 54–60
  chinaware, 56–57
  glassware, 57
  gold plate, 57–58
  hand dishwashing, 54–55, 56
  pewter, 58
  silverware, 58–59
  stainless steel, 59–60
  wood, 60
Tapestry, 80
Tea stains, 116
Telephone numbers, emergency, 15, 123
Television sets, 66–67
Termites, 140–41

Terrazzo floors, 86
Ticks, 141–42
Tile floors
  ceramic, 86–87
  quarry, 87
Tin cookware, 52–53
Toaster-broilers, 34–35
Toasters, 34
Toilet bowls, 39
Tools for cleaning, 8–15
  safety suggestions, 15–17
Track lighting, 44

Underpadding of carpets, 94
Underwriters Laboratories (UL), 16–17
U. S. Department of Agriculture, 5, 122, 123, 124, 128, 136, 139
U. S. Department of Commerce, 73, 81–82
Upholstered furniture, 63–65
  removing stains from, 112–13
Urine stains, 118

Vacuum cleaners, 13–15
  attachments for, 14–15
Venetian blinds, 106
Vinegar, white, 3
  marble and, 3
  for stain removal, 115
Vinyl floors, 87–90
Vinyl upholstery, 64–65
Vomit stains, 118

Wall design hanging fixtures, 44
Wall paneling, 99–100
Walls, 98–102
  bathroom, 40

major cleanup, plan of
    action for, 98
painted, 99
papered, 100–1
removing stains from,
    101–2
Washable plastics, 43
Wash basins, 38–39
Washing (sal) soda, 5
Wasps, 142
Waterbugs, 130–32
Watercolors, 78–79
Waterproof household gloves,
    7–8
Wax-applicator pads, 12
Waxes, 8
Waxing
  cork floors, 84, 91
  vinyl floors, 88
  windows, 105–6
  wood floors, 90, 91
Wax removal, 88–89
Wax stains, 115–16
Wet method of cleaning
    carpets, 93
White vinegar, 3
  marble and, 3
  for stain removal, 115

Wicker furniture, 65
Window blinds, 106–7
Window coverings, 106–11
Window frames, 99
Windows, 103–6
  bathroom, 39–40
  washing, 103–6
Window screens, 110
Window shades, 111
Wine stains, 118
Woks, electric, 33–34
Wood
  accessories 78
  and silver, 77
  blinds, natural-wood,
      106–7
  floors, 90–92
    refinishing, 91–92
  furniture, 61–63
    cleaning, 62–63
    painted, 63
    polishing, 61–62
  tableware, 60
Woodwork, 99
Woven rugs, coarsely, 95
Wrought-iron furniture,
    65–66